THE

Wife-in-Law
TRAP

THE
Wife-in-Law
TRAP

❋

Ann Crytser

POCKET BOOKS

New York   London   Toronto   Sydney   Tokyo   Singapore

To protect the privacy of the individuals who have contributed to this book, all names used throughout are pseudonyms.

 POCKET BOOKS, a division of Simon & Schuster Inc.
1230 Avenue of the Americas, New York, NY 10020

Crytser, Ann.
    The wife-in-law trap / Ann Crytser.
        p.   cm.
    ISBN 0-671-67433-1 : $17.95
    1. Remarriage—United States.   2. Wives—United States—
Psychology.   I. Title.
HQ1019.U6C79   1990
306.84—dc20   90-34135
                                                                        CIP

First Pocket Books hardcover printing June 1990

10 9 8 7 6 5 4 3 2 1

TO
THE WIVES-IN-LAW
WHO OPENLY
SHARED THEIR
PERSONAL STORIES
FOR THE CREATION
OF THIS BOOK.

＊

* ACKNOWLEDGMENTS *

If there's one thing a first-time author needs, it's encouragement—and out-and-out cheering. And if there's one thing that I got throughout the development of this book, it was encouragement—and out-and-out cheering. Starting with a cadre of family members that included my teenage son, Morgan, my two brothers and their families, and my ninety-two-year-old aunt, the invaluable support unit branched out to encompass childhood and current neighbors, old and new friends, and past and present professional colleagues.

Whoever started the rumor that a writer's life is lonely is only half right; for while there's truly no way around the aloneness that is required for putting pen to paper, the rallying of so many friends on this project has made it anything but lonely. I've enjoyed regular calls, cards, letters, and visits from friends, both from all over the country and from my international days in Japan, Singapore, Thailand, Guam, and Bahrain. There have been the friends who have understood my need to be left alone for extended periods to execute the project as well as those (often the same) who have called or stopped by to insist I take a break or those who, I'm thankful to say, have imposed breaks by visiting or booking me on a trip. If cheering alone could accomplish the task, this book would be one of the swiftest and finest ever written, for I have been truly blessed in this area.

Most importantly, of course, The Wife-in-Law Trap is the result of the confidence and commitment of many professionals, and I thank especially these individuals:

Susan Schulman, my literary agent, for her confidence in the book's concept;

Elaine Pfefferblit, senior editor at Pocket Books, who expertly directed the work;

Laura Bellotti and Laurie Levin, for professional writing assistance;

Mary Ellen Durham, ACSW, who led focus group sessions and served as clinical consultant throughout;

Dr. Patricia Amick and Dr. Greer Fox, primary and secondary research consultants; and

Gwen Galbreath, my secretary.

All this support has been extremely heartening, and for all of it I shout a big, "Thanks!"

* CONTENTS *

✳ FOREWORD ✳

I am pleased and honored to have been a part of what I feel is a ground-breaking book. This is the first book to address in depth the unique problems and concerns of the countless women whose ex-husbands have remarried and those who marry previously married men.

When Ann Crytser first shared her idea of *The Wife-in-Law Trap* with me, my initial reaction was that it would be an important cathartic experience for her. The next afternoon as I sat with a client in my office, it struck me that I was listening to a wife-in-law talking about the very issues that are core to this book. I reflected on how many other women I have talked with over the years in my practice who have been struggling with these same issues: intense feelings of pain, love, hate, fear, anger, resentment—and with no rules or traditions to go by. I quickly telephoned Ann and responded eagerly to her invitation to serve as a clinical consultant for this book. I am more convinced than ever, after compiling the questionnaires, conducting focus groups, and talking personally with many women, that her work is extremely relevant to a huge segment of our population.

There are currently more than fourteen million wives-in-law in the United States. The projected growth of this group, based on the remarriages of three quarters of a million divorced men annually, is a million and a half wives-in-law a year. Moreover, one of every two children will experience the wife-in-law relationship at some point during childhood, and tens of millions of extended family members will be affected. Although staggering numbers are involved, very little has been written either from a clinical or self-help perspective regarding the gamut of emotions women experience or the day-to-day problems they face with parenting, money, societal dos and don'ts, boundary issues, and the like.

The Wife-in-Law Trap is about the relationship between women who are unwillingly connected to each other because they've been married to the same man. It's frequently a relationship between adversaries who must learn to become members of the same family.

More than one hundred women, both former and current wives, participated in the creation of this book by responding to questionnaires, participating in in-person and telephone interviews and focus groups, and revealing their own unique case histories and experiences. The stories they tell will resonate for anyone who has ever lived in a family torn apart by divorce and reshaped by remarriage.

As a family therapist, I work from a point of reference that begins with the family dynamic. Since the family system is a delicate balance of individuals, the entry of a new member creates tremendous chaos and uncertainty. The family must readjust its patterns of behavior, and every person in the family usually undergoes a painful growth process. It is my hope that this book will provide significant guidance and insight to wives-in-law and clinicians alike.

The Wife-in-Law Trap begins by explaining that current and ex-wives face the same issues from opposite sides of the emotional fence. The ex-wife must deal with rage and jealousy if her wife-in-law was the "other woman," and in any case often feels rejected, replaced, and overstressed by increased parenting and financial burdens. The current wife, on the other hand, enters her new family with optimism but recognizes early on that she has married not only a man, not only stepchildren, but an ex-wife as well. Her new life encompasses problems and burdens carried over from the former family. Both women must work toward becoming more aware of the other's position, since the better they are able to get along, the more comfortable it will be for all family members.

While wives-in-law may never become friends, it is hoped that with the life stories and guidance provided in this book, they will understand that it is within their capabilities to put an end to painful no-win situations, deal honestly and openly with parental, legal, social, financial, and emotional issues, and move on with their lives. Knowing that they are not alone in this struggle makes it all possible.

The many turbulent emotions and stages that permeate the personal stories here will validate and inspire others facing the same trials and traumas. The conflicts between two women involved in a wife-in-law relationship are often overwhelming, and learning from what other women have gone through can be a life-changing experience.

The Wife-in-Law Trap also addresses the male, mutual-husband perspective, and I believe the book will be beneficial to men also. It will not only enhance their understanding of the tension between their "two wives," but will also show in what ways the wife-in-law relationship is a family affair in which everyone—mutual husband, in-laws, children, stepchildren—is profoundly involved.

The Wife-in-Law Trap provides millions of women and their families the opportunity to identify the source of their pain, work through it, and enjoy happier family lives. I am grateful to have been a part of this valuable project, and I have enormous respect for the women who shared their experiences with all of us honestly and courageously. It is, in fact, their lives that will help us all to grow.

—Mary Ellen Durham
Academy of Certified Social Workers, Diplomate
Dallas, Texas, 1990

✳ INTRODUCTION ✳

Not long after my ex-husband's remarriage, in a rush to deposit my just-received monthly child support and alimony check, I dashed by the drive-thru window of one of the branches of my bank. This particular support check had been written by my ex-husband's current wife, and since I was not on my usual banking turf, the young teller didn't recognize me, my car, my name, or the check drawn on an out-of-state bank.

"Excuse me. Excuse me," the teller's voice boomed too loudly over the microphone and across the parking lot. "Is this check from a relative?" As she mashed the check up against the glass of the window, I found myself self-consciously turning around to see if any of the customers waiting in the cars behind me had heard this embarrassing question.

"A relative?" I whispered to myself. Flustered, I stared back at the teller and mumbled, "My husband's second wife . . . a relative? You've got to be kidding!"

In the course of the next few seconds, though, I began to flash on how much of a relative she actually was. Horrified at the unfolding realization, it struck me forcefully how intertwined and linked our lives actually were. But relatives?

Yes, relatives indeed, bound by a mutual husband, with whom we had both exchanged identical forever-after vows, a bond with the same child, the same mother- and father-in-law, the same sister-in-law, and the same niece and nephew! We share the same last name, some of the same friends, even some of the same property and possessions. She has lived in my house, driven my car, and slept in my bed—with my husband! And, as this moment made painfully obvious, we even share money.

Regaining my composure, I smiled at the young teller and, peering over the steering wheel of my car, I muttered, "That check *is* from a relative—it's from my wife-in-law!"

After almost a decade of having a wife-in-law, I am never completely prepared for the complexity of emotions that are periodically and unexpectedly triggered by some incident that reminds me of this unwanted kinship. In spite of all the good advice I got from friends and all the books I read on handling divorce, I was never prepared to have a wife-in-law. One source of solace has been my conversations with other women who also have "other wives" in their lives. In sharing laughter and anguish over their stories and mine, we established a bond of common experience, and I realized that they weren't any better prepared for the relationship than I. We became soul mates.

At first I naively thought that most of the painful and important issues were the exclusive province of ex-wives. I just assumed that second wives had gone on to live happily ever after. A close friend of mine, who was also a second wife, actually helped me recognize and appreciate some of the anxieties and frustrations from her perspective as a current wife, among them: fielding the anger of the ex-wife, adjusting to the challenges of being a stepparent, and coming to terms with the physical, emotional, and financial implications of that first family in her husband's life.

Once I had heard her story, I realized that my relationship with my own wife-in-law was largely defined by my one-sided assumptions. I was caught in the wife-in-law trap. I woke to the possibility of trying to make sense out of these anxieties, frustrations, and unresolved fears, from *both* perspectives. I sought to understand both sides—the former wife's and the current one's— and wondered if there weren't many other undiscovered elements in this strange connection. After a search through libraries and discussions with professionals, it became clear that this very complex relationship affecting millions of people had never been closely examined. With the assistance of a professional researcher, I set about preparing and distributing a formal questionnaire to serve as the basis for data collection. Starting with a handful of my friends and their friends, the fourteen-page questionnaire was networked to wives-in-law all over the country, and completed questionnaires were received from ninety-three women in sixty-three cities across the nation. The responses represent the perspectives of fifty former wives and sixty-two current wives. Nineteen of the respondents completed questionnaires as both former and current wives (see Appendix).

The respondents ranged in age from twenty-eight to sixty-five. Their marriages spanned periods of a few months to as long as thirty years. Their children ranged from infancy to people in their twenties and thirties; some had children of their own. I heard from women in all walks of life: lawyers, bankers, nurses, housewives, businesswomen, students, travel agents, realtors, artists, and editors. Each woman, living her unique version of this story, offered insights into the range of stages and strategies for dealing with the difficult wife-in-law relationship.

The formal questionnaires were supplemented with data from personal, informal interviews. I spoke at length with a total of sixty-five women, thirty-two former wives and thirty-three second or subsequent wives, either by telephone or face-to-face. With assistance from Mary Ellen Durham, I also organized a series of focus groups in Knoxville, Tennessee, and Dallas, Texas.

At every step along the way I was moved by the candor with which these women shared their stories and opened their hearts. Their interest and concern for the subject was confirmed by their commitment to completing the lengthy questionnaire and taking the time to attach cover letters replete with extended comments. Many women spoke with me for several hours in the personal or telephone interviews, while others devoted many hours to the focus-group discussions.

In the course of our interviews many were curious to know whether the research findings indicated that they were "normal." I concluded that, like myself, these women were seeking a validation of their experiences as wives-in-law and were delighted to find they weren't alone in their experiences or feelings. If there was a single, dominant response I heard, it was, "If only I had had a book like this!" Well, here it is, "a book like this," and it's one that grows directly out of the experiences of the true experts, the wives-in-law themselves.

It is my hope that *The Wife-in-Law Trap* will serve to reassure all wives-in-law that they are not alone in dealing with this often-troubling connection that has been thrust upon them. I hope, also, that it will help to define the unique conflicts and difficulties that each of us faces. By demonstrating how the women in these pages have dealt with their struggles and successes, we can all better prepare for dealing with our own wives-in-law, and with all the daunting challenges of divorce and remarriage.

No One Ever Told Me I'd Be a Wife-in-Law

1 Failed Marriage + 1 Remarriage =
2 Wives-in-Law

I grew up on a two-block stretch of Emoriland Boulevard in Knoxville, Tennessee. It was one of those neighborhoods that was possible back in the forties when dads worked and moms stayed home. There were a dozen or more of us kids within six to eight years of each other's ages who grew up in and out of each other's homes; boys and girls rounding up sandlot baseball games, staging plays, talent shows, and mock weddings, publishing a neighborhood newspaper, and playing tag late into the long summer evenings. There were no "broken homes," no divorces, no children of divorce, no remarriages, no stepfamilies.

The notion of divorce never entered my mind when I married in 1965. When our best friends suddenly divorced in 1970, I realized for the first time that if it could happen to them, it could happen to us. By 1978 I was reading Mel Krantzler's *Creative Divorce.*

A generation later, I know hardly anyone whose life is untouched by divorce and its consequences. The divorce rate in the United States is the highest in the world; it is now around 4.8 percent per 1,000 population.[1] Some research predicts that the rate of divorce is increasing so that two out of every three first marriages contracted in the mid-1980s will end within the next thirty years.[2] The net result is that families are being split and spliced like recombinant DNA.

Every time a divorced man remarries, wives-in-law are created—two by two. According to the latest advanced report from the National Center for Health Statistics, the total number of remarriages in 1986 numbered 632,068.[3] In that one year alone, over a half million ex-wives and an equal number of current wives were created. If your ex-husband has remarried or if you are married to a divorced man, you *are* and *have* a wife-in-law.

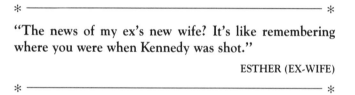

*   *

"The news of my ex's new wife? It's like remembering where you were when Kennedy was shot."

ESTHER (EX-WIFE)

*   *

There is simply no good way of breaking the news to ex-wives that their ex-husbands are about to remarry, or already have. Although most women would prefer to hear the news directly from their ex-husbands, word generally travels by way of emissaries—in-laws, children, friends, or neighbors.

In my case, I learned of my former husband's remarriage from my ex-mother-in-law who was visiting my son and me. She answered the phone one afternoon; the caller happened to be her son. When she hung up, she graciously informed me that he had just gotten remarried. We'd been divorced less than six months and I was outraged and hurt that he hadn't told me himself. It seemed downright cowardly, and I still remember vividly the sting of shock and pain.

But it wasn't until a year later that I really felt the impact of his remarriage. My ex-husband was living in the Middle East and had had contact with me and my son through letters, regular international telephone calls, and visits to our home when he was in the U.S. But I had never exchanged so much as one word with my new wife-in-law. Now my eleven-year-old son was scheduled to visit his father and stepmother for the first time in Bahrain. This meant sending him halfway across the world into a hotbed of political unrest and the care of his father and a woman about whom I knew practically nothing. It struck me forcefully that this stranger would have significant personal involvement in my son's life, and therefore in mine. Watching my child board the late-night plane, I felt alone and panic-stricken—out of control. Through that massive air-terminal window I saw the reality. Like it or not, this woman was my ex-husband's other wife, my son's new stepmother, my very own wife-in-law.

* ———————————————————————— *
"Reality is the best possible cure for illusions."
                                    LILLY (CURRENT WIFE)
* ———————————————————————— *

As children, we all have ideas about how things are going to be when we grow up. They come from the stories we are told, the life we see around us, the values we are brought up with. For me, marriage and children, a world centered around family life, like the families on Emoriland Boulevard, was my future. This vision was reinforced by the most popular television shows of the fifties: "Ozzie and Harriet," "The Donna Reed Show," and

"Father Knows Best" all provided, week after week, year after year, an unlimited supply of safe, manicured, picket-fence images of happy families. The TV wives were immaculate housekeepers and utterly devoted to their children, who were never more than lovingly rebellious or adorably naughty. The TV husbands were often befuddled by the complexity of domestic life, but usually saved the day with sage advice or prudent counsel, as wives looked on, ever-so deferentially, grateful that someone reliable was manning the helm. Between them, TV couples never endured anything more disruptive than an occasional tiff, and even these spats were resolved with kiss-and-make-up good-nights as they crawled contentedly into their starched twin beds to live happily ever after. These flickering images of family life provided the backdrop for my expectations of how my own family-to-be should act and look. It was a vision shared by an entire generation.

Eventually I did get married and for many years my happily-ever-after beliefs went unchallenged mostly because I ignored everything that didn't fit my perfect picture. My view of the world was that families were groups of people related by blood living together in cozy households of parents and children (known now as nuclear families).

When I began to see beyond Emoriland Boulevard, it became clear that not all contemporary families met this limited definition. My marriage mythology told me "once and forever," but a look at all the divorce and remarriage around me told me "once, and then again, and then . . .". This marriage arrangement, which can also be defined as serial monogamy, creates a daisy chain of people extending over space and time. For example, wives-in-law live in separate but intricately connected households with children moving back and forth between the primary parents according to every conceivable arrangement. Many of these families are transgenerational—Dad's second wife may be ten years older or younger than his daughter, and Mom's boyfriend may be twenty years her senior.

These are not traditional families, but they are families

nonetheless: extended contemporary families with their own potentials and their own problems. Those of us who still try to cling to sitcom mythology may on some level be attempting to reconcile our own awkward, extended contemporary family to our former ideals of what family life *should* be rather than what it really *is*, and what it is that needs to change.

This requires perspective, and it's not always easy to see the forest for the trees, especially if you're the one on the tangled path of divorce—a path that is particularly rocky. Wives-in-law are generally planted smack-dab in the middle of the family forest, and relations with them are just one of many thickets we may encounter along the way. If we are lost, we need to scale a tree to gain a vantage point. The journey takes courage, and it can be terrifying at first. But when we reach a clearing, the family forest may look different and we will be able to see our way through all the unnerving life adjustments that come with divorce or remarriage, co-parenting, financial worries, emotional upheavals, and persistent personal doubts. The challenge begins with a deep breath and the hope that things can be different and better once we get a firm handhold on how things actually are.

"Figuring out our relationship is like trying to figure out a beast with six heads!"

PAM (CURRENT WIFE)

Most wives-in-law spend a good deal of time trying to make sense of their relationship to each other. No wonder. There are certain specific characteristics that make this already-fraught union even more vexing. The bottom line is that in nearly every case the wife-in-law relationship is:

- Unchosen
- Unwanted

- Without rules or traditions
- Volatile
- Ever changing
- Permanent

UNCHOSEN:
To begin with, it is highly unlikely that any woman would ever willingly choose to have a wife-in-law. And few women I know who have one would ever have chosen the particular woman that her husband married. But, in real life, since husbands don't ask for their opinion or consent, wives-in-law are constantly faced with trying to come to terms with an involuntary kinship. They are somehow expected to make their situation, however awkward and difficult, work.

Often they have opinions of each other that are based more on hearsay and turbulent feelings than on first hand experiences. The current wife usually knows something about her wife-in-law from her husband long before they meet. The former wife often hears bits and pieces about her successor secondhand from children, in-laws, and mutual friends. Both ex- and current wives are compelled to take what comes "for better or for worse."

When relations between wives-in-law are strained, it may seem logical to look to the mutual husband to take some responsibility since it was his decision to remarry that connected them in the first place. Logical, yes, but unrealistic. Wives-in-law report that husbands typically opt for noninvolvement as a way of handling emotional discomfort when things heat up (we'll talk about this at length in Chapter 7). This usually leaves the women to sort things out for themselves.

UNWANTED:
The majority of women polled in this survey resisted the idea that they were related to their wife-in-law, legally or otherwise. Rather, they felt the connection to be adversarial and intrusive. This is particularly true of former wives who have

children: They live with the gnawing, at times overwhelming, anxiety that their children will be cast aside for the sake of the new marriage and any new offspring. For the current wives, preexisting family obligations are burdensome, expensive, and threaten to stand in the way of their desire to build a new life, unencumbered by the past.

Every child visitation, birthday, holiday dinner, vacation, life event, and alimony check drives home the reality of the connection. First-wife Heather recalled the time she planned a surprise birthday party for her daughter, only to find that her wife-in-law had done the same and refused to reschedule the event. Her little girl ended up being rushed from one event to another in tears. Amanda told me that she and her husband inadvertently booked the same cruise as her ex did with his new wife. "I felt like I was under house arrest," she said with a shudder. "I spent 80 percent of the time in my cabin, either seasick or heartsick." It is a relationship that simply won't go away, that attempts to deny the legitimacy of both positions, polarizing those involved and creating, at best, a standoff situation.

WITHOUT RULES OR TRADITIONS:

None of the modern etiquette books that I've read include chapters on "how to treat your wife-in-law" or on "disciplining your husband's children." In fact, once we go outside the boundaries of the nuclear family and venture into the unmapped jungles of modern compound families, we are in uncharted territory. There are no textbooks, no instruction manuals, no sage advice. If we, as wives-in-law, search for role models, the closest we come are Alexis and Crystal of "Dynasty." More like the Monster vs. the Martyr, they fail to provide a constructive example for real-life solutions, to put it mildly.

The ex-wife leaves the exalted status of married woman, governed by traditions and rules, to enter into the nether region of divorcée. She moves from a marriage based on vows to love and cherish to a divorce based on court orders to divide money, property, and children. The current wife is coming from roughly the other direction. As she defines her married life, she must factor in the obligations and conditions of her husband's divorce. In the face of all the cross-ties and complications, wives-in-law rarely sit down together and work out ground rules; they are far more likely to rely on husbands, children, and other in-laws to act as intermediaries, negotiators, and legislators. Few take advantage of the opportunity to invent new rules where none exist. Without precedents, wives-in-law are left to their own devices. In the absence of cultural incentives and family support, creative resolutions to both immediate and fundamental problems may seem out of reach. (Part of my purpose in writing this book, of course, is precisely to begin to establish some necessary guidelines.)

VOLATILE:

Wives-in-law are frequently required to interact around highly charged emotional issues (children, money, property) often during times of crisis (illness, accidents, financial reversals, death) or celebration (holidays, birthdays, life events) in public places with people they are not necessarily close to. These issues are trigger points that are intensified by unresolved tensions, bittersweet memories, and fragile expectations. Given this powder keg, it's not surprising that the wife-in-law relationship is riddled with irrational prejudices, obsessive emotions, and unpredictable, sometimes outrageous, behavior.

Take me for an example. My ex-husband married a flight attendant; for years afterward I never referred to her by name. I lost all desire to travel to her native country and even bristled whenever I heard her language spoken. And as if this wasn't bad enough, I wouldn't set foot on the airline she worked for, though I knew how childish these attitudes were. After all the venom, however, I am happy to report that this phase is at long last behind me. But it all took time—years in fact.

The primitive and volatile nature of these emotions forms the basis of the wife-in-law relationship. When I asked women to appraise their feelings toward their wives-in-law and assess the latter's feelings toward them, the majority of both ex-wives and current wives identified resentment and jealousy as the two dominant emotions experienced. I became a sounding board for such comments as, "My wife-in-law cashed in when she married my ex and she's about as deserving as Leona Helmsley!" or, "She got the whole enchilada—the big house, the hefty alimony, the new car—and my husband and I are left with the headaches and credit-card payments." To add insult to injury, each group felt that their counterparts were more resentful, jealous, and competitive than they themselves were!

The vast majority of women in our study were deeply curious about the other wife's relationship with the mutual husband. Lita wondered if her ex-husband's taste for saucy late-night videos put as much of a damper on her wife-in-law's sex life as it had on hers. First-wife Gail was dying to find out how Connie, her wife-in-law, was putting up with her ex's outbursts in restaurants. Mira couldn't wait to ask her wife-in-law if she "liked" cleaning a day's worth of trout on her ex-husband's annual fishing vacations.

Current wives, whose husbands have debriefed them on their former marriages, would love to hear their wives-in-law's versions and wonder what would be said, woman-to-woman. Current-wife Sydney had a hard time believing that her wife-in-law's shopping sprees were as extravagant as her tightwad husband described. She wanted to see the Imelda Marcos shoe collection with her own eyes! And Monica imagined lunching with her wife-in-law to find out if Ken, their mutual husband, had always been this difficult to get close to.

These emphatic inclinations are indications of the very real possibility of potential peace between wives-in-law. These "related" women are in unique positions to understand and be sympathetic toward each other's difficulties and trials—if they are no longer slaves to the bitterness and resentment that can blind them to each other's vulnerabilities. In Chapter 8 we will take a look at the different ways wives-in-law have created solutions they can live with. Those who have achieved mutual understanding say that it takes conciliatory and cooperative communication that evolves over time as well as a generous investment of self-reflection and forgiveness. But this kind of openness and generosity seems to come only with time: The healing of these wounds is an ongoing, long-term process.

EVER CHANGING:

If you have contact with your wife-in-law, then it may be safe to say that in some respects it is like any other relationship that evolves and changes. The changing nature of the wife-in-law relationship takes place on two timetables: short-term interactions influenced by daily circumstances and immediate reactions, and long-term patterns that reveal the relationship's overall direction as it progresses positively or negatively. For example, Amanda's relationship with her wife-in-law was slow-growing and incremental but nonetheless demonstrates a significant shift.

I've got sixteen years to talk about. Had you asked me the same questions at intervals five or ten years ago, the story would have been different each time. When I initiated my divorce, my ex moved out of state and refused to have anything to do with me or with Ray, our son, except through our lawyers. When he did remarry, it took me nine months to hear the news. I can understand his hurt but could never accept that he abandoned Ray. To this day I suspect his new wife capitalized on his divorce wounds and discouraged contact with us. Actually, she and I never spoke for the first three years of their marriage.

Then Ray decided to reestablish ties with his estranged father. My ex still refused to speak with me, so my wife-in-law and I had to work out the logistics for the holiday visits. Over time we went from no words at all to brittle messages left on the answering machines. Once she got to care for Ray, she warmed to me and initiated polite but restrained conversations. Gradually, we got used to the reality of each other. As my son grew up and became his own person, he sorted things out directly with his father, and my contact with my ex and my wife-in-law ceased to be necessary. If I were to bump into her now, I expect it would be like greeting a cordial acquaintance, and that's a vast improvement over the glacial treatment she gave me at the beginning.

If we could have the benefit of twenty-twenty hindsight at the beginning of a relationship, we would be able to discover the ways in which things got stuck or evolved. The good news, based on my research, is that wife-in-law relationships can change for the better and, in most cases, tend to become less painful and disturbing over time. Even where there is continuing estrangement or hostility, there can be greater *acceptance* of the situation.

Women learn to shift their position from victim to survivor and begin to move on with their own lives. Children grow up and leave home, minimizing the need for interaction and reducing the tensions that almost always surround financial obligations. An ex-wife remarries. Someone moves to another city. Self-esteem is restored. And time really does heal.

Those women whose situations have not improved implicate a single underlying reason—their inability to forgive. Unresolved issues fester and fuel flare-ups that keep the wounds open. Wives-in-law may fall into a pattern of heaping blame on each other for past grievances rather than sharing the responsibility for things in the here and now. And as we know from the widely available information on codependency, forgiving the other also means taking a hard, painful look within and forgiving ourselves.

PERMANENT:

Wives-in-law are linked through life, even when there are no children involved. When there are, the growing-up years make the ties even tighter, and endlessly binding. And then, just when wives-in-law feel they have made it through the rough times and can finally deal maturely with this prickly relationship, just when they feel they have a new lease on life, something totally unexpected may happen. The ex-wife may lose her job, she may suffer an illness or accident, a grandchild may appear. She may be unable to sever her emotional connection to her ex-husband and may act as if she is still married to him. Old emotions, raw and unresolved, often resurface, ushering in renewed potential for tension and friction. Does this ever end? The answer: a resounding "No!"

Problems of aging, illness, and death can also ignite wife-in-law tensions. An ex-husband becomes critically ill and is not expected to live. His ex-wife is determined to see him once more; his current wife is determined she won't. A poorly drawn will or divorce decree can bind the two women into a beyond-the-grave struggle.

Wives-in-law are eternally connected, it seems—"as long as we both shall live . . . till death do us part!"

First Meetings with HER

Most wives-in-law meet long before death spares them the trauma. Knowing you have a wife-in-law is one thing, seeing her in the flesh is quite another! For most of us it's much easier to maintain emotional equilibrium when she has no corporeal existence. But once you've experienced your wife-in-law face-to-face, it's virtually impossible to wish her away.

Not surprisingly, these moments are spiked with white-knuckle fear, killer anticipation, and obsessive curiosity. Women describe those first meetings as "intimidating," "bone crushing," and "monstrous." First encounters are indelibly etched into our memories in great detail. "Every time I get a whiff of Giorgio perfume my mind faxes me a copy of that day—in living color!" quipped one wife-in-law. Indeed, most of the women I spoke with have total recall of the day, time, place, and what they were wearing when the moment occurred.

It's a moment for which we are seldom prepared. Although wives-in-law accept the inevitability of an encounter and try to plan for it, few take place as expected. We don't look the way (as good as) we thought (hoped); we blank out on the responses we'd mentally rehearsed. And we are all too often caught off guard by our own flood of emotions.

The early encounters are rarely easy, and the ex-wife is particularly vulnerable. If she ended her marriage unwillingly and hasn't remarried, confronting the reality of her husband's new beloved is wrenchingly tough. First meetings are dominated by overwhelming emotions like searing jealousy, bottomless insecurity, and naked rage. Even the most levelheaded woman, like Trudy, is susceptible:

> Hank and I had been sweethearts in high school, and we married shortly after his junior year in college. We were in the bloom of youth, but after twelve years of marriage both of us had gotten a little ragged, especially me. Our divorce, or I should say *his* divorce, wasn't easy. It took me a long time to recover, and four years later, when Hank said he was going to remarry, it threw me for a loop. I went into a hole for months and I kept bugging Hank to introduce me to Trish, my successor. I imagined her to be everything I wasn't, and I somehow needed to prove it to myself, even if it meant that I'd be miserable. At least I would be right.
>
> He never brought her around even though I continued to ask to meet her. Then, one day it just happened. I kept saying to myself, "At least now she'll be real."
>
> I was working around the house that afternoon. Hank, Trish, and the kids had been away for Labor Day, and they suddenly pulled into the driveway. After

eight hours in the car, Trish hops out in perfectly pressed linen shorts with every hair on her head in place. I felt like Godzilla facing Venus. It was the first time I had seen them as a couple, a family. I thought I had a grip on it all, but when I went back into the house I cried for that entire night. I can't describe the loneliness, the unhappiness. I was convinced that no one would ever love me again. I felt used up, discarded and ridiculous.

Current wives aren't spared the agony either. Sometimes a "reputation" as a husband-stealer precedes them. Sometimes they inherit the unfinished business of the former marriage. Many times current wives find that their husbands are implicitly asking them to defer in various ways to the first wife out of guilt feelings or a need to keep up appearances. Beverly, a second wife, found herself feeling jealous rage in this situation, and with good reason.

Sam's ex-wife always believed that I broke up his marriage, and it's something that Sam hasn't done a good job straightening out. In fact, it's been a bone of contention between us. All I know is that he's got a lot of guilt about the divorce, so when he sees Paula, he's extra-syrupy sweet and puts her on a pedestal to compensate. In many ways she is not out of the picture. We live in the same town, so I was determined to act like a lady if we ever met. I was going to be gracious or die trying. Shortly after our first anniversary, Sam and I went out for dinner and ran into Paula and her friends in the doorway of a restaurant. It was Paula's birthday and she was with a group of friends who'd known them both before the divorce. I was introduced, but before we could break loose we'd been invited inside for drinks. For the next hour, Sam, Paula, and their friends reminisced. I was invisible while Sam was being overly solicitous to Paula. He kept saying, "I hope you're having a lovely birthday." She was in the limelight and I simply faded away. Tears started running down my face and Sam finally realized that I wasn't just going to disappear. I've tried not to hold it against her, but she continues to hold center stage to this day. I think that evening set the tone for what has come afterward.

But not all meetings are ill-fated. Current-wife Marianna met her wife-in-law for the first time after ten years of marriage at her stepson's high-school graduation. The anticipation had been enormous.

Amelia, Bob's ex, and I didn't get off to a great start ten years ago. Bob didn't want to tell her that we were getting married. So on the Friday before our wedding he asked if he could pick Joey up a little early, and could she include some dress-up clothes in his overnight bag. When she found out what was really happening, she was furious. Understandably, things weren't smooth after that. Even though we had never met until Joey's graduation, the passage of time had managed to ease things a bit. Still, I planned ahead and thought about what I was going to wear. As Bob and I drove onto the campus, I took some deep breaths, but my heart was still pounding. Amelia and her husband were seated, so I had a chance to see her before she saw me. She looked lovely! As we walked up, there was an awkward moment with everyone checking everyone out. Joey came running up with his girlfriend and gave us all bear hugs. He helped to bring us all back to why we were there. The photographs are wonderful—our graduating son, parents, their spouses, everyone grinning ear to ear.

Actually, I learned something from Amelia. Her

marriage to Bob bore a lot of the same problems ours now does. She survived the breakup and raised a son single-handedly. Frankly, she's done one hell of a good job. She is a far cry from the "bad guy" that Bob made her out to be.

Unlike Marianna, most of the women in this survey had already met their wives-in-law prior to their new relationship. Some had been casual social acquaintances; others had been former close friends, neighbors, and college roommates. Many had had previous involvement in each other's lives—for example, as co-workers, spouses of co-workers, hairdressers, teachers, swimming instructors, or baby-sitters.

Needless to say, women who became wives-in-law under these circumstances were hard-pressed to maintain their ties, and a fragile coexistence often took the place of friendly relations. In rare cases, bonds of friendship developed into what can only be described as truly extended families. Perhaps if we look to these extraordinary instances, we can find some clues to managing our own wife-in-law relationships.

Leann and I go back to high school together. We both served on the yearbook staff, and we were pretty good friends. When we met again some fifteen years later at our reunion, I was married to Dave and she was just getting out of a seven-year marriage, with two kids. Dave decided to fix her up with his divorced law partner, Tom. We even double-dated a couple of times. Tom and Leann ended up marrying and moving away. Six years later she moved back to town alone. By that time, Dave and I were separated. After we split we spent a lot of time understanding why and working out with a marriage counselor some of the reasons we couldn't live together anymore. There were still a lot of loose ends, but we were both ready to walk away from the marriage and say we'd tried our best.

Dave looked up Leann about two years into our divorce. His office needed a paralegal and she needed a job. It was a perfect fit in more ways than one. The rest is history; they were married three years ago.

There was a time I would have gladly ripped her head off, but the children have been the glue that held things together. Dave and I have three kids about the same age as Leann's. One of hers and one of ours are in the same grade at the same high school, so we were constantly being thrown together at school events. At one point we just fought it out. I think it was about the car-pool schedule. There was a cooling-out period, and then we decided that we just had to find a better way. Life was just too complicated if we couldn't depend on one another.

It began with a family reunion that we planned together. We felt like a tribe so we figured we might as well act like one. I wouldn't go so far as to call us co-wives, but we are working on being co-mothers. That's not to say there aren't occasional bruises and bumps. The pain is still there but it's not the center of attention any longer. Leann and I have gone on with our lives somehow. I went back to school and became a lawyer, which was a major factor in helping me reestablish myself.

When we are together now we aren't punishing each other for what we thought was being taken away. Instead, we keep an eye on what is in place, what is positive and important in our lives.

Harriet (ex-wife)

What clues does Harriet's story provide? First, Harriet and her husband had found a way of making amends that put to rest many of the more troubling issues in their failing marriage. Second, after Dave remarried, Harriet and Leann were quick to realize that their lives and their children's would be a lot easier and more pleasant if they could cooperate. Third, both women acknowledged their difficulties, fought it out, and jointly decided to invest the time and effort to make their relationship work as best they could. Fourth, each created independent lives that fortified their self-esteem and gave them the strength to face each other and their mutual problems. And fifth, when things got rough, they continually refocused on the opportunities rather than the losses a compound family could offer.

In the chapters to come, we'll run the gamut of horrifying to heavenly wife-in-law stories, each with its own peculiar set of tragedies and triumphs. But first, let's explore some of the inner workings of how wives-in-law think and react, depending on what side of the divorce and remarriage experience they are coming from.

2

Opposite Directions

Probably the most profound personal decision we make is the decision to marry one particular person. This allegedly once-in-a-lifetime choice embodies our deepest feelings of love and commitment, as well as years of hopes and plans and dreams. Our promises to ourselves and our chosen mates are solemn ones indeed. Ironically, the one thing we have in common with our wife-in-law is that we both chose the same man to marry. Granted, we chose him at different stages in our lives and his, and perhaps for very different reasons. Nonetheless, we made a very similar decision concerning something of deep and lasting significance. Paradoxically, it is this profound similarity that divides us and sets us up to become adversaries.

There are many paradoxes connected with being and having a wife-in-law. We are alike, yet we are polar opposites. We are rivals or enemies, yet we are part of the same family. We never chose to be connected to one another, yet we probably will be for life. Since our relationship is so often fraught with ambivalence and pain, perhaps our first step toward clarifying our positions and alleviating our discomfort might be to acknowledge our unique roles in this unusual kinship.

The Former Wife

No matter what the circumstances of the failed marriage or the terms of divorce, ex-wives come into the wife-in-law relationship from a position of loss: lost love, lost dreams, lost home and hearth, lost financial security, lost friends, lost relatives. Whether we feel guilt and regret for having given up on a marriage, or profoundly rejected by a mate who gave up on us, the sense of loss is devastating and painfully compounded by the assumption that someone else is succeeding where we have failed. Thus, ex-wives characteristically enter the wife-in-law relationship feeling wounded and emotionally drained.

With our marriage dreams a thing of the past, we ex-wives face new challenges, frightening challenges which frequently include full parental responsibility, diminished financial resources, and a self-image often in dire need of rebuilding. Perhaps we feel others blame us for the failure of our marriage. Perhaps we blame ourselves. And in addition to the burden of guilt, we often feel left out and isolated as single women in a couples world. We sense shifts in the loyalties of our friends and in-laws, and come face-to-face with the greatest fear of all—that we will be forced to share our children's affections with a wife-in-law who may care for them too little or too much.

The fears and concerns that ex-wives voiced most frequently in our discussions together centered around four basic issues:

- the loss of identity as a consequence of being replaced by another wife
- the feeling of having been discarded by the former husband
- the sense of having been cheated out of the rewards of marriage after investing years, energy, and love

- the need to compete with a wife-in-law for the love of one's own children

Each of these issues makes it clear that for ex-wives, their children, and their families, life will never be the same. No matter what their background or surrounding circumstances— even for women who appear to have calmly walked away from exhausted marriages—ex-wives are victimized by a society that favors couples and stigmatizes divorce.

Divorce, even when you've chosen it, is a difficult enough transition; but when an ex-husband remarries, we are not only divorced but replaced. We face yet another traumatic blow: Someone else has assumed the position we once held, increasing our already acute sense of lost identity. Ex-wife Trudy felt as though she had actually walked out of her own life while her wife-in-law stepped right into it.

I feel like my wife-in-law has taken my place not only with my husband but in all the activities that used to make up my life and that I can no longer take for granted. The country club my husband and I used to belong to, the medical auxiliary functions, my ex-sister-in-law's annual Fourth of July party—I'm just no longer welcome at any of those places.

My wife-in-law has even taken over some of the friendships I used to think were so special. Friends my husband and I had known for years—most of them just seem to avoid me now. It's like I have to create a whole new life for myself. It's very difficult, but I know that I have to deal with it. I feel very hostile toward her when I realize that my options have diminished while hers have increased. I know my marriage wasn't perfect—in fact, I was pretty miserable most of the time—but I can't see that she'll be any better a wife than I was. And when I think about how she has a chance to start over with my husband, it drives me almost insane! Why didn't he give me a second chance?

Trudy's struggle is one that countless ex-wives grapple with. None of us likes to feel disposable. We are all unique, multifaceted, evolving individuals with very specific lives to live. Yet our self-esteem is all too often based on other people's—especially our mate's—treatment of us as well as on circumstances we cannot control.

When our marriage falls apart and our husband embarks on a new one, many of us use the event to flagellate ourselves: "If only I had been more . . ." or, "His new wife is so much younger and prettier, how could I expect him to still love me?" or, "Why was *he* the first one to find someone new—why couldn't I have remarried first?" The fact is, marriage is a complex and difficult relationship to sustain. Trying to figure out what went wrong with yours and why it's going right with his and hers isn't at all simple.

What does help is to try to come to a deeper understanding about what was wrong *and* right in your previous marriage. Not everyone realizes it, but marriage counselors also help ex-couples understand their failed marriages—not only so that they can have a clearer picture of what went wrong and learn from past mistakes, but so they'll be able to remember and acknowledge what was good and valuable in their former relationship. We all need to salvage some positive memories from previous alliances in order to forge strong new ones. And as preposterous as it might sound to get into counseling with your ex, many couples attest to the personal benefits of finally coming to terms with their former spouses. They say they tend to dwell less obsessively on the past once they understand it.

We can never expect to let go of our past entirely, nor can we realistically claim to be rid of the devastating effects of a marital breakup after a given number of weeks, months, or years. The shock to our emotional systems is often much greater than we care to acknowledge, and we're called upon to make certain psychological transitions for which we're usually unprepared. Continuing to value ourselves after being rejected by a mate is certainly not easy. We may express anger, but what we're usually feeling is hurt, loss of self-esteem, loss of trust. We can reach some resolution with these difficult, unhappy emotions, but we can't expect to bounce back overnight. We need to learn—or relearn—to treat ourselves with love and respect. We need to acknowledge our pain and insecurity, but also trust that the darkest days will eventually pass.

Lauren's story reveals how, even when we've reached the point where we're finally moving ahead with our life, certain reminders from the past can force us to reexperience the shock and hurt of being "discarded."

After my divorce I was eager to leave my old life behind me. I packed two suitcases and, with my young child, headed halfway across the world to start a new life.

When I learned my husband had remarried, I was immediately determined to regain possession of some of the artifacts we had accumulated in the course of our fourteen-year marriage. I figured that neither my ex-husband nor my new wife-in-law would be particularly interested in having these reminders of me around the house anyway.

When I asked my ex-husband to ship the collectibles to me, he agreed. The day the goods arrived it felt like Christmas—a packing crate of my very own things that I hadn't seen in over a year!

I began working with the hammer to open the crate and see what surprises it held. Joy of joys, there was the antique four-drawer chest my husband and I had purchased some fifteen years earlier. It was a simple, rustic chest but I had always loved it. I couldn't have been more pleased. I tested the drawers to make sure they still worked, and in the top drawer were a few odds and ends: knitting needles, wood-carving tools, and a half dozen or so music books. I was feeling happier by the minute. These were all things that took me back to very happy times in my past, and I was touched that my ex-husband and his wife had slipped them in the drawer rather than just tossing them out. Then, I opened the second drawer and found . . . a set of old, threadbare white sheets! I went berserk! The warm feelings I had just experienced were instantly replaced by craziness. I had an image of my ex-husband and his new wife standing on the steps in front of their house (our house! my house!), hands cupped around their mouths, shouting, "Here! You forgot your sheets!" Talk about forever being reminded that you'd been discarded and replaced . . . with the bedsheets shipped out behind you!

That was ten years ago. I've often thought about those old sheets. It could all have been just a mistake, but no matter. To me those sheets became a symbol— and their shipment to me a symbolic gesture—a tangible reminder that I had, indeed, been replaced in my marriage bed.

Humiliation, abandonment, a sense of being unjustly cast aside—none of us anticipates such circumstances or emotions when we marry. In the early glow, most of us consider our husbands as our partners, our best friends, our chosen mates with whom we'll share the best and the worst life has to offer. We're in it for the duration, otherwise we wouldn't have gotten married. We imagine we'll progress in our careers, have children, buy a house, build toward the future, watch our grandchildren grow, and live contentedly ever after. The frustrating scenario for many former wives is that they participate in the early years of struggle and sacrifice, and then find themselves torn out of the picture when it's time to reap the rewards and benefits.

How many of us have helped put a young husband through

school only to be left for another woman once he is ready to launch his career? And how many marriages have lasted until the children left home, at which time a wife of twenty-some years is left by her suddenly "dissatisfied" husband? Former-wife Frances voiced her resentment over having given "the best years of her life" to building a future she was no longer entitled to claim.

> Charlie and I got married when we were both in our early twenties. I worked as a secretary until the kids were born, and then I did odd secretarial jobs part time at home. Charlie struggled pretty hard also. His sales job required that he put in long hours in order to really get ahead. But neither of us complained, because we were looking to the future. And there was a lot of love there—at least in those early days. It took a long time before things turned around financially, but we finally "made it." And then, as soon as we did, Charlie decided he wanted a divorce. Talk about timing! We had jobs we liked and financial security. We had a good life, a home we had worked hard to build. We had everything going for us, and suddenly, overnight, Charlie was gone—and so was my life. He and I had worked together all those years, and now my wife-in-law not only has him, but she's also reaping the benefits of *my* labors. I feel so cheated, yet there's no way I can ever really be repaid, since it's so much more than just the loss of material things.

How does a former wife like Frances begin to find compensation for all she's lost? Perhaps the first step is to allow herself to feel the hurt and disappointment. As unlikely as it may sound, when we give in to the normal feelings of loss associated with death, separation, or divorce, and let ourselves experience them, we actually suffer less in the long run. That doesn't mean we ought to wallow in those emotions endlessly, but we shouldn't deny them or feel bad about grieving over what we can't reclaim. Once we have come through that grieving process, we can begin to take stock of what we *haven't* lost.

In Frances's case, she had more going for her than she was ready to acknowledge at first. She had two wonderful kids who were loving and supportive. She enjoyed a close relationship with several longtime friends. And she had also developed some very marketable skills during the years she and her ex-husband were building toward their future. In fact, she had become a top-notch word processor and administrative assistant—and eventually landed an excellent job as an executive secretary with a prestigious public relations firm.

Still, there's no way Frances can be "paid back" for the love and commitment she gave to her ex-husband. She says she'll never be able to understand his brisk decision to end their marriage, nor does she see why he finds his new wife to be a better mate. But she hasn't given up on herself. She's in a Divorce Anonymous support group, from which she derives very concrete benefits—the greatest of which is learning that she is not alone in her emotional trials. She's beginning to make new friends, and is now planning for the economic changes she must make as she begins a new life.

While every loss associated with divorce can be wrenching, we do make adjustments, and in time a new life does begin to emerge. However, one thing that cannot be negotiated is our relationship to our children. Former wives frequently experience enormous anxiety when they think they might be losing their child's affection or that their maternal role is being usurped by a wife-in-law. Amelia articulated this greatest fear of ex-wives: losing their children's love.

> I guess I was prepared for all the obvious losses. I had lost my mate, and to some extent my social position. I know my wife-in-law is much better off financially than I am. She's the one taking the fancy trips and redecorating her home while I'm pinching pennies. But one thing I wasn't prepared for was my five-year-

old daughter coming to me one day and saying, "Oh, Mommy, Mara makes the best fried chicken, and we had so much fun planting a garden together. I can't wait to go back next Saturday."

I'm not too fond of my wife-in-law—for all the obvious reasons—but I must admit, she has a wonderful way with children. She's very creative and is childlike herself. I guess that's good and bad. She's also younger than I am, and very pretty, so it was understandable that my little girl, Janie, would like her. Yet I actually found myself hoping Mara would lose her temper with Janie or do something to make Janie like her less. I'm almost ashamed to admit it, but I suffered a lot thinking Janie might come to love her stepmother as much or more than she loves me.

It's a terrifying feeling, but I felt like I was competing for my own child's love. I did stupid, frantic things to try to be inventive, funny, entertaining. I went overboard until I realized I couldn't force my daughter's love. I finally gave all that up and got back to trying to have a real relationship with her.

Actually, a child can only benefit from receiving more love—if it's genuine. It's normal for mothers to feel competitive with stepmothers, but we can learn, with patient effort, to overcome that rivalry by thinking about what's best for our children. Will it really be such a bad thing if our daughter loves her stepmother? Will she really love us any less? In fact, what might make our kids appreciate us less is their sense of our compulsive competitiveness with their stepparents, because we tend at such times to be our worst selves. Children need us to be our familiar, reliable, loving selves. It's very much to our benefit to focus on our own lives with our children rather than to compare ourselves, favorably or unfavorably, to our wives-in-law. It may feel like a frightening loss when our young daughter is delighted with her new stepmother, but, in fact, how can her added happiness detract from our own?

Faced with the pressure of so many real or imagined losses, it's no wonder that in the early years of the wife-in-law relationship ex-wives are hurt and resentful, even vengeful. Ex-wives told me of the extreme behavior they contemplated at bad moments. They fantasized wrecking their wife-in-law's car, stealing her clothes, or spying on her in an aerobics class. One former wife told me she actually felt like using the new couple's bed as a trampoline and jumping up and down on it when she had an occasion to be alone in their home.

Fortunately for both former and current wives, the vengeful phase does pass eventually and may even be looked back on with humor in time. It's natural to feel resentful and competitive, yet ultimately most former wives I talked to became survivors who were committed to putting their lives back together. Although there were many moments of discouragement along the way, many experienced the satisfaction of being able to readjust their lives (sometimes more than once). Going back to school, taking on a new career, learning more about themselves, developing new interests, reaching out to new friends, or meeting a new man were all ways in which ex-wives began not only to put their fractured lives back together but to actually reshape them, often into a stronger form.

Shaken by changes most of them had not anticipated or desired, they refused to be destroyed by those changes. Even a young woman whose husband had deserted her and their three young children and then married someone even younger had the inner resources to declare, "Life is good. I have been able to develop peace of mind after all that's happened. I never wanted the divorce, but as it's turned out, this is the best thing that could have happened to me. I've gotten to know myself, and I'd go through it all again to be where I am today."

The Current Wife

If the former wife's emotional state is generally one of loss, the current wife's is usually one of hope. The current wife's vision is dominated by the promising future, not the shattered past. She is suffused with the glowing belief that everything will work out. With a new husband, often a new family, and a new future, the second wife looks forward to a set of challenging new priorities.

One thing a second wife doesn't particularly look forward to, however, is cultivating a relationship with her husband's ex-wife. Given her choice, she would undoubtedly have chosen a man unencumbered by a prior marriage. On the other hand, some second wives believe that previously married men make better husbands because they "know the ropes" and have, they hope, learned from experience. In fact, a 1987 study indicates that second marriages have a somewhat higher probability of failure than first marriages, with 37 percent of second marriages among women terminating within ten years as compared with 30 percent of first marriages. Among men, the comparable figures are 31 percent and 27 percent respectively.[1] Yet, rather than question the wisdom of marrying someone who couldn't make a previous marriage last, second wives tend to be optimistic and believe they can succeed where someone else has failed.

As we all know, optimism and hope count for a lot and may even make it possible to transform a difficult relationship into a compatible one. But even with hope and optimism going for them, new wives have their own new struggles to deal with.

Current wives told me that their basic concerns were:

- feeling like an outsider who has to prove herself
- dealing with the emotional and psychological baggage of the earlier marriage
- taking on the responsibility of being a stepmother

If a husband has children from a previous marriage, the current wife must resign herself to sharing her mate's available time and affection. She never feels really entitled to that honeymoon phase of being completely alone with her new spouse. In fact, a second wife's courtship can include the presence of his kids as early as the first date! Even when he is childless, he can have financial, family, or psychological ties that will bind him to his former wife for years to come—or for a lifetime.

If a second wife doesn't have complicated money issues keeping her awake nights (How will her husband be able to fund *his* two kids through college as well as contribute to *their* son's private elementary school education?), she's probably plagued with fears that her wife-in-law will never remarry, that their mutual husband will never quite forget his first wife, or that she herself will never fully adjust to living in the shadow of a previous wife and family.

New wives must gain the acceptance and goodwill of step-children and in-laws who are all too often predisposed to resent and disapprove of them. They must fit into a social scheme which had previously included the ex-wife, to whom the new wife will most certainly be compared and judged accordingly. In other words, a subsequent wife is always the second act, and the first wife can be a hard one to follow. Louise talked about the difficulty she had winning her stepchildren's trust, and how their avoidance of her made her feel like an outsider.

Whenever there's a crisis in my husband's "other family," it invades my domain, whether I want it to or not.

His ex-wife recently had surgery—they thought she might have a recurrence of cancer. Of course her children were very upset. At the same time, she was trying to elicit help and advice from my husband, who was trying very hard not to get involved with her. There was a period of a couple of weeks when all these problems were in my house—unspoken, but there. I was hurt that my four stepchildren didn't feel close enough to me to share their concern about their mother. I wanted to help them, be available to them, but I didn't want to appear intrusive. It's a difficult balancing act; it really is.

Although there are those stepmothers who competitively try to undermine the former wife, or who overmother their stepchildren as compensation for never having had their own, most don't want to upset their stepchild's relationship with the birth mother or in any way "take her place." What they usually *do* want is to be friends with their husband's children and to care for them without stepping on anyone's toes. It's a delicate balancing act, indeed, and the consequences of failure are highly intimidating. Caring for children who aren't your own but who are a continuing part of your life can be one of the most trying— yet one of the most rewarding—aspects of being a second wife. It's no wonder that second wives are beset by feelings of anger, frustration, and ambivalence, especially since they cannot look to a future time when they will have their husbands completely to themselves and to their mutual children. The intrusion of the former family is something they must simply come to accept. Stacey's story illustrates the mixed feelings associated with becoming a member of a ready-made stepfamily.

> I really got cold feet before our wedding. And it was all about the boys. It dawned on me that by marrying Matthew, I was also getting involved with two kids, and I didn't know how that was going to go. Not only would I have to share my husband, but I'd be taking on a tremendous responsibility I hadn't really considered fully. I kept thinking that if my husband were to get run over by a truck when we'd been married only a week, I'd still have some kind of connection to his kids throughout my lifetime. And that was just real scary to me. In the five years of my marriage, my life has been closely entwined with the lives of my stepsons, and to a large extent I'm happy about that. Yet there's no way I could possibly have anticipated how much their lives would affect my own.

Stepchildren aren't the only obstacle a current wife faces in her quest for marital happiness and tranquillity. On a very practical level, there are financial considerations which are generally problematic. These may be as relatively simple as the mutual husband's need to continue covering the former wife's car payments, meaning that the current wife may have to sacrifice by driving her well-worn jalopy for an extra couple of years. Or there may be far more complex situations to deal with. For instance, a former wife may still be named in a mutual husband's will or may be designated to receive a portion of her ex-husband's pension, shares of stock, and/or life insurance policies. Children from the former family may have college funds that are substantially contributed to on a regular basis. Such financial obligations to former families may seriously undermine a current wife's own family finances and plans for the future. She may even find it necessary to consult with a lawyer to assure herself that grave financial pitfalls will be avoided.

Community property and inheritance laws vary from state to state. But in California, for example, the first wife continues to have a share in all deferred compensations, such as pensions and life insurance policies, even if her husband divorces her and remarries. Pensions and insurance policies are considered to be community property, and, if for instance the first wife was married to the mutual husband for twenty years, she receives, on his death, a prorated share of all the assets accumulated on those policies, based on the number of years they were married. Again, this is the general case in California, and current wives with similar financial concerns might want to discuss the matter with their husbands and/or contact an attorney for information specific to their own home state.

Equally, certain psychological and emotional issues connected with the former marriage will in all likelihood need to be dealt with in the context of the second marriage. If the former couple had problems with communication or sex or conflict resolution, chances are they didn't learn how to solve those problems before the marriage ended. So a husband may, consciously or unconsciously, carry into his new marriage these former marital conflicts. Perhaps the former couple were never able to discuss their differences without resorting to anger and name-calling. Or maybe one partner habitually withdrew, leaving the other to nag the silent one until the disagreement escalated to crisis proportions. Sexual incompatibility may have gone undiscussed, leaving both partners feeling hurt and insecure. Whatever the scenario, the mutual husband will often transfer his past marital difficulties to his new marriage. Annie explains how this dynamic works in her own marriage.

> Sometimes when I fight with my husband I can feel my wife-in-law's presence. He has certain problems relating to the people he's closest to, and those difficulties really surfaced in his former marriage. Basically, he has a very hard time expressing his feelings, and his ex-wife used to come down on him a lot for that. I have to admit I agree with her. I get terribly frustrated trying to reach him and read his various moods. But I try to be straightforward with him rather than critical. Even so, sometimes I think he'd just prefer to be on his own, with no obligations and no need to share his feelings with a wife. I think he and I are beginning to have a much more open relationship, and we're working on things in therapy, but sometimes I wish I had waited longer to marry him so that he could have had more time to work things out before jumping into another marriage.

So, as we've seen, unresolved problems may be displaced onto the current wife, even though they may have absolutely nothing to do with her. One current wife told me her husband refused to allow her to have her own credit card, for fear she would run up exorbitant bills (a bad habit his ex-wife never broke), despite the fact that she was extremely frugal. But that had little impact on her husband's tendency to associate her with his ex-wife's shopping addiction.

Hannah also talked about how conflicts from her husband's first marriage became problems of her own:

> I think my husband still resents his ex-wife. He tends either to idealize me and set me up as her complete opposite or, when there's an argument, to respond to me as if I had her motivations. When you marry someone who's been married before, that former relationship never really goes away. You're not just marrying a man—you're actually marrying him and his former wife—all the problems they shared when they were married get transferred to your own marriage.

As we've said, second wives know all too well that their divorced men come as "packages," with ex-wives, children, financial responsibilities, even ex-in-laws and ex-pets, in tow. Even so, they're never quite prepared for all the consequences of their unique role. It often requires a great deal of inner strength to "share" a husband with those who came before you, to face the stigma of being "the other woman" even when that label doesn't apply, to live with a man whose past brings to bear so many emotional complications, to make the kinds of financial sacrifices some other wives are never called upon to make. It's a good thing second wives begin their marriages on a wave of optimism: They will certainly need it to deal with the challenges ahead.

So Who's Blaming Whom?

It's clear that both ex- and current wives find themselves with a multitude of circumstantial and emotional dilemmas to sort out. But the specific problems they create are very different, depending on whether one is wife number one or wife number two.

Wife number one is fearful that her children won't be in good hands with their new stepmother—or that they'll come to love her more than they love their own mom. Wife number two is fearful her new stepchildren won't accept her, will hold her responsible for their parents' divorce, or will simply be too much of a drain on her new marriage. A former wife worries that she won't be able to get along without two incomes. A current wife worries that too much of her husband's income is being siphoned off to pay alimony and child support. A first wife misses the friends she and her ex used to socialize with. A second wife feels insecure about whether those same friends will accept her. Former wives experience divorce as the most stressful upheaval in their lifetime; only the death of a loved one is more devastating. Second wives feel the aftershocks of the former marriage's emotional convulsions. They must live with the husbands whose ex-wives now feel rejected or insecure or guilty or embittered, men who often have plenty of unresolved feelings themselves.

So while our struggles are interconnected, our problems are different. And our personalities and backgrounds differ as well, as do our perceptions of ourselves and of our wives-in-law. In fact, 60 percent of the survey respondents said they saw themselves as different or "complete opposites" from their wives-in-law (even though some believed their husbands married a "different version of the same woman"). Yet, do these differences— real or perceived—necessarily predispose us to conflict? There are, of course, second wives who were directly involved in the breakup of the former marriage. In this circumstance, it is only natural for the ex- and current wives initially to feel only bitterness and rivalry toward one another. But even women who weren't in that thorny situation felt overwhelmingly bitter and competitive toward their wives-in-law.

Much of the anger former wives felt toward their ex-husbands was often displaced onto the current wife. Rather than discussing explosive issues directly with their ex-husbands, former wives took it out on their successors, with feelings and actions of intense hostility. They inwardly protest, *How can he prefer her to me? How can he still love our children so much and not love me anymore? How can he say he cares about being a father when he heaps all the parenting responsibilities on my shoulders? How can he leave me stranded financially? How can he do this to me?* But instead of crying out to their ex-mates, former wives used every opportunity to butt heads with their surrogate enemies—their wives-in-law.

On the other hand, it seems that many second wives have a tendency to let mutual husbands off the hook, to blame ex-wives for marital and postmarital difficulties. They want to believe the best about their husbands, so they try to ignore their wife-in-law's perspective.

When asked who they thought was responsible for the failure of the former marriage, ex-wives tended to blame the husbands; they rarely saw themselves as active participants in a disastrous relationship. Current wives tended to blame ex-wives for the divorce. Few second wives saw their husbands as responsible parties in the breakup, and so seldom asked themselves why they had chosen someone who had been unable to hold a previous marriage together. It is all too human to want to place the blame for failure anywhere but on ourselves. And in most instances, especially where two people have struggled to make a go of a marriage and have failed, the responsibility is a shared one. So we should not blame only ourselves. But in order to assess our relationships realistically, we do need to begin by taking responsibility for our part in them. When we do so, it becomes easier to determine the roles of the other players, how things went seriously wrong, and how we can move into the future without making the same mistakes over and over.

But we need to do more than look to the past to become more comfortable with our place in this new expanded family. Divorce and remarriage create a triangle of characters with three distinct yet connected sides. We need to acknowledge these connections and understand their distinguishing features. We need to begin to view the triangle of former wife/mutual husband/current wife from all possible angles. The relationship of ex- to current wife is more complex than "you versus me" or "right versus wrong." Our struggles cannot be weighed on an emotional scale with our wife-in-law's having no value and ours having it all. We need to identify with her point of view, imagine ourselves in her shoes, in order to gain deeper insight into a volatile set of interrelationships.

We must do all this to make the wife-in-law relationship work *for* us instead of *against* us. If we can become objective enough and honest enough, we may reach the point where each member of this unplanned extended family can finally begin to feel comfortable relating to one another.

3

For Better, for Worse

Within the space of two short years, Bonnie was faced with the sudden departure of her husband, an ugly divorce, life as a single parent, the shock of the almost immediate remarriage of her ex-husband, explosive confrontations with her young wife-in-law, and the announcement of a baby soon to be born to the happy new couple. "What more can I take?" Bonnie pleaded. "I've had it!"

Bonnie has had more than "it," she's had a megadose of most of "them," the eight key factors which affect the nature and quality of the wife-in-law relationship:

1. Children
2. The Other Woman
3. Resolution
4. Remarriage
5. Territory
6. Timing
7. Personality
8. Satisfaction

The interplay of these factors shapes the unique ebb and flow of each wife-in-law relationship. As the circumstances surrounding each one change, so does the rhythm of cordiality or conflict between former and current wives.

CHILDREN:

When no children are involved, the lives of wives-in-law are simplified considerably. Most women report that contact with their wife-in-law is minimized, and sometimes even eliminated altogether, if they do not have to deal with the issue of child care. Conversely, the *single* most important reason that wives-in-law relate at all is children. They must deal with children born into the current union or the former one(s), or with children or stepchildren of previous or subsequent marriages.

Children are the pivotal point that determines whether or not there will be highly charged issues between wives-in-law. The intensity of the charge depends, to a large degree, on:

- the age of the children
- how many are present in the shared households
- where the children are in their emotional development
- the kinds of concerns they have about their parents' divorce and remarriage
- the synergy of family personalities

Each woman brings a certain level of emotional maturity (or immaturity) and a set of needs to the equation. I spoke to mothers who longed to share parenting and to stepmothers seeking to co-parent. Rarely, however, were they paired wives-in-law. More often, the ex-wife seeking to share parenting was contending with a wife-in-law who was hostile toward her and her children. Just as typically, the stepmother seeking a more active role in caretaking was rebuffed by a wife-in-law who expressed her desire for control through strict visitation rules.

The blending of families, as we will see in Chapter 4, is a critical juncture for the entire compound family. Children are the incentives for compromise between wives-in-law; just as often, they are the ostensible reason for discord and dissension. How this issue is dealt with often symbolizes the residual pain and unresolved conflict the adults themselves still carry.

THE OTHER WOMAN:

Not surprisingly, the sense of betrayal is deepest when the other woman was closely associated with the couple before the divorce. Not only do ex-wives feel bitterly betrayed by their husbands, they also begin to doubt themselves and their own judgment. The lingering question is twofold: How could my *friend* have done this to me; how could I have been so blind? Wanda and Gail know this scenario only too well.

Kim and I were friends well before my husband even knew she existed. As neighbors, we'd have chats in the afternoons, swap favors and exchange car-pool days. One day we came up with the idea of cooking Friday-night gourmet dinners for the four of us, her husband and mine. That led to playing some mixed doubles on the weekends.

Kim and Herb, my husband, got very good as partners and started competing in tournaments. They even played city-wide one year. We were all having a grand old time. I was completely caught up with the *image* of my marriage. All my attention went to managing the house, our social lives, my job, and the children. My husband was starved for some tender loving care. I didn't have time to be his buddy, but Kim did.

Meanwhile, Kim and I began to see less and less of each other alone—no more afternoon talks. When she started having a difficult time looking me in the eye, I thought it was because she was going through tough times with her husband and felt self-conscious

FOR BETTER, FOR WORSE

about sharing her pain. I didn't ask because I figured it wasn't any of my business. I never suspected a thing.

Although Kim and my ex swear left and right that they never had an affair until the divorces were final, it's hard for me to believe. I don't speak to either of them and haven't for the last six years. Everything is handled through our lawyers except for the messages that Annie, my eldest daughter, carries back and forth. I can't believe I didn't sniff out the signs. To say I feel foolish is an understatement. But more than that, I lost trust in myself. How could I not have seen what was before my very eyes?

Wanda (ex-wife)

I will never forgive Connie for breaking up my marriage. She was set on luring Ted away from me if it killed her. When I found out about the affair, I almost killed both of them. Ted and Connie met through business; she was the account executive on a project he had in Chicago. My husband would go there for business twice a month for a few days at a time, all prepared with the fresh shirts I had laundered in the suitcase I had neatly packed.

I would never have found out if he hadn't left his briefcase in her office. It was returned to our house on a Saturday by overnight mail, all official looking in its corporate envelope, except it was addressed to "Teddie" instead of Ted. That was the tip-off. When I asked him about it he immediately switched the topic and started complaining that I had allowed the romance to go out of our marriage. I began to laugh and then he got real serious. He said that we had some problems that he couldn't live with any longer. I was getting a lot of double messages. We had just gone through a period of closeness but the truth of the matter is that he *had* been acting funny for a while. I kept ignoring it, hoping it would go away. I never quite had the courage to discuss it with him directly, and he never mentioned anything either. That night was no exception and we went to bed silent.

The next morning when I woke up he was downstairs. Out of nowhere he told me he was moving out. I asked him if he was involved with someone else and he kept denying it. That night he packed up and left for Chicago. My gut told me that he was seeing someone else. I looked up the return address on the express package. It was marked Chicago, as were the American Express restaurant charges from his "business trips." Bingo! Connie's name kept coming up. I was so enraged that the only thing I could think to do was get to Chicago.

The next day I stormed into Connie's office and demanded an explanation. She must have been afraid I'd do something violent because she confessed right away. My worst suspicions were confirmed, but at least I didn't feel crazy anymore.

That was the first and last time I saw my wife-in-law, thank God. It takes every ounce of decency in me to let the kids near either of them during the summer visitations . . . that's as close as we ever get.

Gail (ex-wife)

Current wives who were the "other women" suffer recriminations not only from ex-wives and in-laws but often also from their own consciences. Guilt feelings persist and weigh heavily on their wife-in-law relationships. Living under this dark shadow, these women must make their own personal reckoning and build relationships with children, in-laws, and friends based on these inglorious beginnings.

If I'm really honest with myself, I was the other woman. It's not something I'm proud of, and I have a lot of guilt to this day. For the eight years that I've been married to Bruce there has been this little voice inside of me that keeps on saying, *Maybe you were being selfish . . . maybe you should have stayed away.*

Right from the beginning, the love that Bruce and I have for one another felt real, but at the same time, it seemed like a no-win situation for everybody. There were too many people who were going to be hurt—and were, especially Bruce's youngest who was only three when he left.

I remember writing Sally a note early on. I said I knew it was probably worthless to tell her this, but I had never wanted to hurt her and I was sorry. She never responded.

Every now and then I think that if I hadn't been there, they might have reconciled. But the reality is that Bruce's divorce would have happened even without me in the picture. Sally is sure that I started trouble, but things were brewing long before. It's just that neither of them had the guts to face the unhappiness. My presence simply made it all obvious to both of them.

RESOLUTION:

For the longest time I just wanted to pretend I could put the pain of my divorce in a Ziploc bag and toss it in the nearest trash compactor. You know, eliminate all the garbage of my ex-marriage—the howling fights in front of the kids and those stone-cold nights in bed when I could hear them crying but couldn't cry myself. I can't let go of those images even though it's been five years since the divorce.

Recently, I read something by the novelist Margaret Atwood, who said, "A divorce is like an amputation; you survive but there is less of you." That just about sums up where I am in making peace with mine. A part of me is gone forever, and that is that.

Maris (ex-wife)

Depending on how ugly and bitter the breakup, ex-wives, postdivorce, are more inclined to feel vengeance and anger than closure and resolution. So the whole idea of bringing divorce to a successful conclusion may sound like a contradiction in terms. And for most ex-wives it is, at first. Like the pain in a phantom limb that feels as though it's still part of our body, the hurt of an unhappy marriage and a turbulent divorce is still sharply felt for many ex-wives. When we are in the throes of reexperiencing our torment, it's easy to believe that it will be this way forever. And indeed sometimes it is. For once the initial wound is healed, mistrust often lingers, and for good reason.

In our culture the legal end of a marriage comes with the last court appearance and the divorce decree. But there are no cultural rituals that help us, our ex-spouses, and our children to mourn collectively and bring to conclusion the *emotional* breakup of a marriage. In most instances we are left to our own devices to conjure up our own expressions of closure: One ex-wife burned all her ex-husband's love letters and anniversary cards; another sold her diamond engagement ring, took the cash, and joined a video dating service; and still another gathered her family and in-laws together for a quiet picnic to thank them for their unfailing support. These may seem like token acts, but to the wives-in-law themselves they are deliberate and necessary affirmations crafted specifically to mark their transition from wife to ex-wife.

At the same time that they are recovering from the divorce trauma, ex-wives must learn to endure their new identity as "divorcée," a designation with about as much going for it as "fallen woman." Stripped of social status and fighting for financial and social survival, many ex-wives end up with chips on their shoulders that they carry for years.

Resolution is further complicated by incomplete or inequitable divorce settlements. Court decisions are usually framed in win/lose terms and each of the divorcing parties often ends up feeling that he or she has come up with the short end of the stick. So, in many cases, the stage is set for continuing struggle. Ex-wives who feel their marriages ended in emotional and financial imbalance may seek to redress it by unremitting litigation.

In addition, if there is bad blood between the divorcing adults it's likely to poison the well of family relations. Usually no one is spared—ex-spouses, children, current wives all suffer. Wives-in-law agree that the parting spirit of the earlier marriage can set the course for future relationships. Sometimes there are so many residual problems after the divorce, such as child custody, support payments, division of property and delegation of liabilities, that making peace with a wife-in-law is simply out of the question. The ex-wife can't be expected simply to turn the other cheek if she is getting the shaft from her ex-husband, and the current wife shouldn't have to wash her wife-in-law's and husband's leftover laundry.

In an ideal situation, confrontational ex-spouses might consider working through major differences in therapy together. Failing this admittedly unusual option, current wives say that their marriages have improved immeasurably when the mutual husband seeks counseling on his own to resolve these leftover issues with his ex-wife. Refusing to let go of the past and move ahead into the future can cripple all affected parties for years as the following account illustrates.

When I think back to those first years after the divorce, I see myself feeling like the Glenn Close character in *Fatal Attraction*. I was so full of hatred and rage for Bobby, my ex-husband, that my fantasies swung between killing myself (to pay him back for the hurt) and killing *him*, which always seemed like a better idea.

Remember when she boils the child's rabbit in the movie? Well, I had this recurring revenge fantasy of skinning Bobby's prizewinning Japanese bobtail cats and pinning them to his door. Gruesome and embarrassing to admit, but true. I was obsessed with retaliation. It took up a lot of time and energy, but I found that playing out all the possibilities over and over got the torture out of my system.

Then he remarried and that set the whole thing in motion all over again. Except that this time I directed all my anger at his prissy-perfect wife, Selma. When I saw her driving a new Cherokee, I knew it was time to go back to court to up my measly child-support payments. The kids were dragged into the fray and even testified at one point.

Even though I got a more favorable settlement the second time around, it still didn't make me feel any better. I finally got it through my thick head that it wasn't just the extra money I was fighting for. I was fighting for Bobby. The glitch was that they weren't going to break up just because I made scenes about what she was getting and what we had to do without. Just the opposite. It made their alliance against me even stronger.

Meanwhile, both my kids were always acting like a full-time UN peace-keeping force in Lebanon, and it was taking its toll. Jenny, my seven-year-old, brought it all home to me. She said, "Mommy, keeping you, Daddy, and Selma from yelling at each other is too big a job for me—I can't scream as loud as you grownups."

That weekend, I took off my wedding ring for the first time in twelve years. It was time to do some reckoning.

REMARRIAGE:

Most current wives long for the remarriage of the former wife. If I heard it once, I heard it a hundred times: "God, how I wish she'd marry again!" The main reason, of course, that current wives are enthusiastic advocates of a first wife's remarrying is that it usually means that alimony payments will cease. An ex-wife's remarriage may also assuage a current wife's guilt, particularly if she believes that she played some part in breaking up the first marriage.

Remarried ex-wives attest that beginning a new life with a second husband helped them to better deal with the wife-in-law triangle. Finding another man who loved and cherished them made them feel more fulfilled and less bitter and vindictive. Not always being the "odd woman out" was enormously helpful in restoring their often shattered sense of self-esteem. Ex-wives no longer felt drained and humiliated by trying to get emotional sustenance from an unlikely source—namely their ex-husbands.

All the women in this survey agreed that if a first wife made a good remarriage, overall relations between wives-in-law improved significantly. Both current and ex-wives corroborate: "When you are happier inside, you don't go looking for ways to make yourself or others unhappy." Emily seconds this observation in her own story.

> I just got married again, and I can feel the difference already. My self-confidence is back, and my relationship with Louise, my wife-in-law, has lightened up quite a bit. Well, actually, *I've* lightened up. A lot of time went by when I didn't date and had no intention of ever getting married again. The truth is that for a long time I didn't want to let Dan off the hook. Our alimony settlement wasn't all that much, but whatever it was I was determined to get it from him for as long as I could.
>
> Letting go of our marriage has been a slow, agonizing process. At the beginning of Dan's remar-

riage, I would do crazy things like drive by their house to see if I could see them through the living-room window. Nuts—I was really nuts, and what a sad waste of my time it all was. With Andy in my life I have a much healthier focus . . . I'm concentrating on us instead of them.

What's really funny is that *I* now have a wife-in-law. I've got to deal with Andy's ex-wife and his children. So I'm learning a lot about what Louise had to go through with me. I'm not so angry with her anymore for having something that I thought was out of my reach . . . a new life with someone I love.

TERRITORY:

Territoriality is an instinctual part of the human animal. Personal boundaries are defined physically, emotionally, and socially, and wife-in-law turf battles are no exception. No matter the size or value of the disputed territory, it's the crossing of boundaries that raises wife-in-law hackles.

Myrna and Isabel both laid claim to an antique Chinese vase that arrived as a gift from an overseas business partner of their mutual husband, who wasn't aware that a divorce and remarriage had taken place. Priscilla and Shana squabbled over the manicurist they both used. Ursula and Madge got out the heavy artillery over a pair of diamond Deco earrings that were willed by their mutual husband's mother to "my son's wife." And, in a particularly sensitive case, an ex-wife had received a special anniversary present from her husband two years before their divorce: a breast augmentation. It had been their little secret. When a friend of both the ex- and current wife asked the ex-wife for the name of her plastic surgeon some four years later, she was certain that her ex-husband had leaked the news and that her wife-in-law was spreading the word.

While some boundaries are explicitly articulated and clearly understood, others are implicit and assumed. We all carve up our worlds into what is ours and what is someone else's, and wives-in-law are master map-makers! "My neighborhood, my super-market, my beauty shop" may be a state of mind, but in cases where tensions are already running high, expropriations can lead to nasty skirmishes.

Ultimately boundaries are established, free zones are agreed upon, and rules, both spoken and unspoken, are accepted or tolerated. Hillary, a current wife, provided an example.

Jill, my wife-in-law, wouldn't let Jerry alone. Every day she would call him about some little thing or another. We'd be in the middle of dinner or spending some time in the evening alone and the damn phone would ring. For example, one night she called to ask him about the kids' homework assignments. Another night she phoned to let him know that she'd taken Buster, their dog, to the vet. She *had* to talk to him—it was almost as if she were pretending he was still her husband.

This bothered me enormously but I decided to be diplomatic. I told Jerry how much I valued the little uninterrupted time we had together and that Jill's unannounced calls were an intrusion. He told me that when they were married she would call him up to eight times a day with every little detail that had come up since he left the house. All those phone calls, he assured me, were "business as usual."

"Then talk during business hours," I said, and we started talking about how much I looked forward to our after-dinner time. Jerry hadn't realized that and was flattered. When I told him that I wanted our romantic time together, he got the idea and bought it! I insisted that he ask Jill to make her calls to him before six-thirty. It's the first step to weaning her away from the habit, and I'm willing to bite the bullet for a while.

I'd love Jill to get it through her skull that *I'm* married to Jerry now and she's not. He's the one that has got to lay down the law, but the first step is to let Jerry know where I draw the line.

Actual physical distance between wife-in-law households also affects the ways in which the territorial factor plays itself out. Most women with whom I spoke agreed that the more breathing space between themselves and their wives-in-law, the easier life became.

If one woman moves across town or to another city, state, or country, it releases both women from the nagging social reminders—constant queries such as, "Which one of David's wives are you?" or, "Are you Nicole's sister?" Distance eliminates the tensions of joint appearances at school, community, and religious activities and frees mutual friends and relatives from loyalty decisions. Wives-in-law who don't have to worry about trespassing on each other's territories find it easier to re-create their social identities and become freestanding individuals, free of each other's auras.

On the other hand, the greater the distance between them, the less motivation or opportunity they have to work out any problems in their relationship. It also makes visitation rights for children more difficult to fulfill. Indeed, pulling up stakes and leaving with the children can be a strategy used to punish an ex-spouse. One current wife told me that her husband's financial support package stipulated that his ex-wife remain in the same city until their son reached the age of eighteen. The ex-wife chose to ignore this part of the settlement and moved five hundred miles away. The second family fought back and managed to get custody of the child. Their struggle became an ugly tug-of-war with the hapless child caught in the middle.

As physical distance between ex-spouses increases, co-parenting becomes more complicated, and sometimes impossible. Although some wives-in-law claim that long distances between the families made extended visits more likely, others talked about the impossibility of truly sharing the unique joys of a child's development that are the rewards of day-to-day responsibility.

TIMING:

Timing, many believe, is everything. It is a convergence of events, some planned, some random, that creates the framework in which the wife-in-law relationship develops.

The relationship between wives-in-law is affected by all sorts of timing: the elapsed time between the first marriage, divorce, and remarriage; the age profile of the principal adults and merging family members; the serendipity of physical and emotional health; the ups and downs of financial and social stability; the evolution of personal and spiritual growth.

In that we all resist change to some extent, I doubt that there are ever "good" times for life-transforming events, especially crises. There seem to be only *bad, worse,* and only very occasionally *better* times in terms of our abilities to deal with stressful changes.

Wanda got the news of Herb's involvement with Kim, her friend and neighbor, upon returning home from her brother's funeral. Certainly *extremely bad timing.*

At least three women in this survey had children under the age of two when their ex-husbands remarried and moved away, leaving them as sole caretakers. Definitely *difficult timing.*

Gail's husband, Ted, walked out a few months following what she described as a close and happy summer and only two weeks after they had moved into the house of their dreams. *Terrible timing!*

When bad timing gets worse, one of the most important things to remember is that the interminable crisis will end—even when there appears to be no end in sight—and that the unrelenting bum luck will change, even when the deck seems most heavily stacked against you.

First, try to take some time-outs—five minutes, an hour, an afternoon—to take some deep breaths and calm yourself down. If we can quiet the emotional chaos for a little while, we can hear our best guide in times of trouble—our own inner voice—which is often lost over the din of anger and accusation. With discipline we can learn to hear it in spite of all the loud interference. With practice we can begin to explore and define our own emotions in the protective privacy of our own thoughts.

Second, when your inner voice comes in loud and clear, take a personal inventory; knowing our own vulnerabilities and limitations points us to our strengths; respecting our weaknesses leads us to self-acceptance and growth.

Third, refocus on defining what the important issue is *now*, and try to avoid dredging up old grievances or creating doomsday predictions for the future. With a clearer picture of what is in our control and what isn't, what we want and what we can settle for, we can avoid feeling overwhelmed and ineffective.

And finally, reward yourself for surviving one more day on the stormy high seas of life! You probably know what is most relaxing for you in times of great stress; even little things can sometimes make a big difference. I guarantee that if you do something nice for yourself, you'll have more energy for the struggle. Find your special something to restore and refresh your frazzled nerves, like Zina, who takes a nice long bubble bath, or Claire, who treats herself to a play or symphony, or Wanda, who goes for a spirit-cleansing swim.

Of course these remedies won't make the problems go away, but they will give us some temporary relief and create an opportunity to get one step closer to clarifying our situation and even finding more workable solutions in the long run. No easy task, but achievable with time and patience. Ask Rena, who has had plenty of practice getting beyond her breaking points.

When I am on the "verge," I'll get into my car and drive to my favorite park, nearby. I have a special bench near the flower garden, where something is always in bloom. I start by taking some nice deep breaths, like the women who do Yoga on TV. Once I've allowed myself to take in the perfection of a rose or the blue of the sky, I ask myself at least one of my four cornerstone questions: Why am I hurting over this? What is it that I really want? What am I willing to give up to get it? What am I willing to offer to make it happen? I make a mental note of whatever comes to my head first and if I have the luxury of time, I will mull over each question until I have the answer that *feels* right.

When I get back into the car, I might scribble my answers down on a piece of paper so I don't forget.

Now, there are times when I can't find the answers to all my questions. But I usually leave that park bench with at least one more piece to my puzzle, and the confidence that I can find another one the next time around. And if nothing else, I've felt the sun on my face and given myself a chance to breathe.

Give it a try; you've got nothing to lose but a few moments on a park bench all to yourself!

PERSONALITY:

Most of us like to imagine that we can get along with just about everyone—with everyone, that is, if our wife-in-law is the big exception. "We mix about as well as oil and water," chuckled one wife-in-law. "She's almost as offensive as the Exxon spill in Alaska! I can't stand her perfume, she has a laugh like a longshoreman, and she thinks that just because she has an MA from some la-di-da college that it makes her a Rhodes scholar. If I were being kind, I'd say we have a personality clash."

Personality clashes come in all sizes and shapes, and if yours takes the form of your wife-in-law, the pressing question may be, "How on Earth am I ever going to tolerate her and still stay sane?" Since the likelihood that we will be able to change *any*, let alone all, of her perceived flaws is just about nil, the "how" depends on whether we can deal with the personality flare-ups with maturity, learning to respect another's point of view and her right to hold it.

So finding a way to relate goes way beyond whether our wife-in-law is snotty, or too businesslike, or short-tempered, and whether or not we approve of her behavior. Our ability to tolerate other people and the way they present themselves to the world is, in part, related to how we feel about ourselves. Paradoxically, the more we expect and insist that people share our values and behave as we do, the less likely we are to really like ourselves—and that's the last thing we ever want to believe! If we don't like and respect ourselves, we usually become very skillful at hiding that awful truth from everyone—including ourselves. When we become skillful at the cover-up, we can have a hard time rediscovering our buried selves. Becoming more tolerant of ourselves can lead to more patience with our wife-in-law also.

Not uncommonly, some of us use numbing destructive behaviors such as substance abuse, child abuse, or even wife-in-law abuse to avoid the pain of self-hate. In the wake of a divorce, hate rears its ugly head in many forms and disguises. By then, a more introspective look at who we are really punishing, and why, is long overdue. Sometimes it takes a startling wake-up alarm—a divorce or the inheritance of a wife-in-law certainly qualifies—so that the glare of reality allows us to see what's really been going on or whom we've become.

Some women in this survey began their personal journeys by looking at the difficulties they were experiencing with their wives-in-law. Many spoke of the importance of seeing how their past responses shaped their reactions to events in the present. In several instances they were able finally to identify dysfunctional parts of themselves as reflections of their own parents' dysfunctional marriages or divorces. These women's struggles to free themselves from repetitive patterns that were no longer working for them took sheer determination and courage. Seeking personal change is an arduous and painful task, but it is an essential beginning. Once these women had faced up to themselves, they

were freed to examine and improve their lives and their relationships to their wives-in-law. Rachel speaks for many who have
heroically accepted the challenge.

When my own parents divorced, my mother drove my
father away. I've seen him exactly once in twenty-
eight years. I am like her in so many ways that I was
terrified of repeating her reaction when Mick and I
divorced. But it wasn't until he remarried that I really
saw it beginning to happen. I was set on undermining
his new wife, Vivian, and was a bitch on wheels. Every
chance I could I tried to poison the kids' minds into
believing that Mick and Vivian were just waiting for
the day to split and leave them high and dry. I had
been abandoned . . . why couldn't the same thing
happen to my kids?
    Mick and I would get into yelling matches about
the kinds of things I was saying about Vivian. One
night he threatened to move out of state just so he
could get some peace. I became hysterical, but somehow I could suddenly hear my mom making mincemeat
of my dad. I knew that if I kept it up I would set in
motion the very thing I so desperately wanted to avoid:
Mick would leave and I would be raising our four
children by myself.
    I just knew I had to take an honest look inside
myself. What I saw was someone who didn't like
herself very much. I blamed everyone else for all the
bad things that were happening. It wasn't easy, but I
had to look at why I had made Vivian the villain, the
enemy, the scapegoat. I felt like she was the winner
and I was the loser all over again. I realized that my
rage was about the father I had lost and the mother
who had driven him away. . . . It had nothing to do
with Vivian at all.
    When I thought about it, my wife-in-law had

taken a lot of my shit and even done it with a measure of dignity. I began to remember how much she cared for our eldest son, John. When he would come home from college we'd all go to the airport to meet him. John would come off the plane, and Vivian would always step back and let me give him the first hug. That showed a real generosity on her part, but the last thing I would ever have done was thank her.

The first bridge I built with Vivian was to let her know that I had noticed that consideration. You have to tell people when they do something that makes you feel good. It took me a long time to screw up the courage and self-confidence to look to the constructive part of our relationship and to openly acknowledge her. Talk about eating crow . . . but it's been worth every mouthful!

SATISFACTION:

Finally, when all is said and done, the essence of the wife-in-law relationship pretty much boils down to whether each of the women got, are getting, or expect to get what they really want. Nearly every woman in our research said she had wrestled with the issues of power and control expressed in trivial battles over who got the silverware, or in deadly serious ones over who won custody of the children.

Women in this survey rated themselves and their wives-in-law in three satisfaction dimensions: financial, social, and sexual—how they reconciled the shortfalls with the triumphs, the disappointed expectations with the realized goals.

An overwhelming majority of current and ex-wives agreed that the current wife holds a distinct economic advantage over her predecessor. Married and unmarried wives-in-law alike believed that women are better off financially when they are wed. The popular TV show "Kate and Allie," which portrayed two struggling divorcées and their children joining forces to create one viable household, reflects many women's reality: Divorce is, all too often, the beginning of financial struggle.

In terms of social satisfaction, however, nearly half of the respondents, both current and ex-wives, indicated that their social positions had improved. But keep in mind that 56 percent of the ex-wives had remarried. Of those who hadn't remarried, nearly three times as many ex-wives, as compared to current ones, stated that their social standing had worsened. These women clearly viewed divorce without remarriage as a less desirable state both socially and financially.

Current wives and ex-wives were of a single mind, overwhelmingly and enthusiastically, in their opinion that their sex lives had improved since divorce or remarriage. Samantha revealed something to us that she had never told anyone before.

I spent the last four years of my marriage in sexual Antarctica. The most physical contact I had with Josh was if we bumped into each other in the hall, even though we were still sleeping in the same bed up to the bitter end. We both suffered from total sex shutdown . . . a result of all of our unexpressed anger plus being bored to death with each other's bodies. Early on in our marriage, I started faking orgasms regularly and got so good at it that even now I can't tell you the last time I had a real one with him.

When we divorced I was scared to death I was frigid. Things had gotten so bad that I started thinking it would be easier to avoid sex altogether than face going through my act with still another unresponsive man.

So I just went about my life like a cloistered nun until I started taking an art class at the community college. When we came to the study of live male nudes—this part embarrasses me every time I think of it—I started getting these unexpected tweaks and twinges. At first I actually thought I must have been coming down with the flu, but a few wild fantasies later I realized that I was simply thawing out. It had been so long since I'd seen a rippling body, and, aside from the exquisite tension of just looking and not touching, I caught myself lusting from afar where it was safe and private.

By the time I met and started dating Zack, I was permitting myself to be interested and curious again about how I would feel if I were with another man. The first time we made love the earth didn't move, but some of the almost-forgotten pleasures started coming back to me—the smell of a man's hair, and being so close to him that you felt you could breathe with his breath. He turned to me afterward and said that he'd never met anyone so sensual, so in touch. I just started to cry. I had been so afraid that those parts of me were gone forever.

I'll be eternally grateful to all those nameless hunks who literally brought me back to my senses. They don't call it "life drawing" for nothing!

Bonnie, Rose, Hillary, Rachel, and Samantha represent only a few of the courageous wives-in-law dealing with one or more combinations of the eight key factors that influence their relationships with themselves and their wives-in-law: Children; The Other Woman; Resolution; Remarriage; Territory; Timing; Personality; Satisfaction. If you are in the midst of trying to untangle your wife-in-law relationship, take a moment to reflect on each of these factors as they apply to your own life. See which of these women's stories holds special significance for you. They may help you discover the sources of your own wife-in-law entrapment. These women found the strength and resilience to move toward greater freedom and well-being; so can you.

Kids Caught in the Middle

When there are children, these children are invariably the number-one concern in the wife-in-law relationship; they are *the* issue. Overshadowing all conflicts, they are the catalyst for confrontation as well as the motivation for cooperation. Kids who get caught in the cross fire of the divorce/ remarriage struggle are not only the children from the former marriage, but those from the subsequent marriage, the current wife's previous marriage, the former wife's subsequent marriage— and sometimes others as well. The cast of characters can be overwhelming and complicated, as are the attendant problems and concerns.

A former wife experiences:

- fear that her own children will take a backseat to those who live with the mutual husband—whether they are his kids from the current marriage or hers from a previous marriage
- resentment toward the current wife's kids and the time and money spent on them

- jealousy over her children's friendship with the step-mother
- jealousy when her ex-husband fathers a child in his new marriage
- anger at being left out of certain child-rearing decisions

A second wife feels:

- upset at the intrusion of stepchildren into her new marriage
- hurt over not being accepted by her stepchildren
- anxiety or resentment over having to take on responsibility for stepchildren
- frustration over the need to scrimp on time or money for her own kids
- sadness if her husband decides he doesn't want a second family

The current and ex-wife both:

- complain about the other's parenting skills
- are overwhelmed by the details of visitation rights
- agonize over thwarted attempts to be a blended family
- experience anxiety over questions of inheritance
- worry about the emotional price the children involved must pay

For the Sake of the Children

In the best of all possible worlds, wives-in-law, their mates, and kids would all meld into one happy, blended family: yours, mine, ours, hers. Everyone would love, respect, and feel comfortable with everyone else. Such families do exist, but they are far more the exception than the rule. When we encounter them, they either inspire us or make us feel envious that we can't achieve a similar level of fulfillment. We wish things could be made easier, more relaxed, more rewarding—and less traumatic for our children. But how is that possible, given all the conflicts that are created when people divorce and remarry?

Most of us, alas, don't live in the best of all possible worlds. Difficult as it may be, a guiding principle by which we must all come to measure our behavior toward our wives-in-law is whether or not our actions are in our children's best interest. Is it really worth it to program our kids to hate their stepmother, when it only means they'll be unhappy with her? Does it make sense to bad-mouth our wife-in-law in front of *her* children? Should we be angry and defensive when our wife-in-law seems to be "out-parenting" us?

Former-wife Bonnie talked about how her wife-in-law (who has no children of her own) takes charge of certain parenting responsibilities and criticizes Bonnie for falling short as a parent. Although Bonnie's son clearly benefits from his relationship with his stepmother, Bonnie finds it difficult to suppress feelings of rivalry.

> I know my wife-in-law is making up for the child she never had. And I guess I feel sympathetic to some extent, but she is going to have to face the fact that Justin is not her son, he's mine. She darns his socks, sews little patches on his blue jeans, makes sure his clothes are all washed when he comes back home, gets his hair cut—all those little motherly touches. Sometimes I think she just does these things to show me that I need guidance in how to be a mother. She even went so far as to write me a letter telling me that she thinks I let my son stay up too late, that I don't get his hair cut often enough, that I haven't taught him to take proper care of his glasses. What really riles me is that she refers to my son as "our son," meaning my ex-husband's and hers. I get an actual pain in my heart when she speaks of Justin as her own.

Bonnie's difficulty in incorporating her son's stepmother into her own notion of "family" hits at the heart of the wife-in-law dilemma. It is completely normal for a former wife to suffer considerable anguish when another woman controls how her children are treated or cared for—especially when that "other woman" is a sexual rival who has usurped her marital position. It's understandable that a former wife would agonize, "How can this person act as if she's my child's parent when she's not? How dare she insinuate herself into *my* family?" The emotional struggle is an intense and painful one.

After a while, though, most former wives do find it easier to separate their own feelings of jealousy and resentment from their desire to do what's best for their children. Because the fact remains that this "other woman" has now become family to their own children. And difficult though it may be, a former wife must gather the strength to encourage a positive, workable relationship between her child and his or her stepmother. Knowing that her son or daughter will ultimately benefit from her efforts makes the task profoundly worthwhile.

Accepting advice about parenting from your wife-in-law is one thing, but what if she actually inhibits you from being a good parent? What if what's best for her child interferes with the well-being of yours? When wives-in-law see themselves as rivals and are unable to jointly resolve mutual parenting issues, they often end up pitting stepchildren against one another, rather than considering each child's specific needs.

Second-wife Yvonne was faced with having to choose between the welfare of her two stepdaughters and that of her own two-year-old son.

> I feel like an intruder in my own home when my stepchildren come to visit. My husband says I even act differently when his kids are here—like I'm walking on eggshells.
>
> My two stepdaughters come with very specific directives from their mother. I'm not to discipline

them or use them as baby-sitters for my two-year-old boy, their half brother. I can't let him play outside with them, because they've been told by their mother that it's not their place to keep an eye on him. If I join them, the girls feel like they're being spied on.

I've been bending over backward to please my stepchildren and comply with my wife-in-law's rules, and to do that I've had to be unreasonably restrictive with my own child. What's really sad is that we're not a family of three, and we're not a family of five either. I hold back from treating my stepdaughters in ways that would make us all feel more like a real family.

Yvonne's situation is particularly sad because so many lives are adversely affected. Yvonne is unhappy and stressed out as a consequence of having to juggle the two sets of children. Her stepdaughters can't be very happy with things as they are since they're so obviously cut off from Yvonne and her son. Spending the weekend with their dad and his new family is probably not something they look forward to, but it would be far more pleasant if their mother allowed them to have a comfortable relationship with their little half brother. And the two-year-old's experience would certainly be enhanced if he had the opportunity to interact more normally with his new stepsisters.

Again, it's normal for Yvonne's wife-in-law to resent Yvonne as her "replacement," but it's unfortunate that she has let her bitter feelings spill over into the lives of the three children involved. If Yvonne were to try to communicate openly with her wife-in-law, telling her exactly what she told me about how difficult it is to keep the children in two separate "camps," the girls' mother might realize how much happier the kids would be if they were allowed to interact as family and might change her behavior accordingly.

Finally, Yvonne and her husband must begin to exercise their parental authority. They need to sit down with the two girls and explain to them that, while their mother has rules which apply in *her* household, Yvonne and the girls' dad also have rules, which apply when the girls are in *their* house. They might explain that those rules include sharing in certain responsibilities—cleaning up after meals, making their beds, and helping to take care of their half brother on occasion. The girls will actually feel less confused and more secure knowing that their father and stepmother are taking a stand and have authority in their own home. It will also make the girls feel more like members of the family, which is, after all, their right.

This question of "who's in charge" comes up frequently in wife-in-law households, and it's crucial that children know that *both* households have a parent or parents who set limits and make rules. Kids need *all* their parents to be parents—to be firm, consistent, and loving. That doesn't mean kids can't be part of the rule-making process, but it does mean they'll be less confused about which parent is in control, and when, and they will be less likely to try to play one set of parents off the other.

None of this is easy. Despite our knowledge that our children may benefit from being integrated members of two households, it can be painful to surrender them to the second family—especially when we feel hostile toward our wife-in-law. Our reluctance to set aside our bitterness leaves our children feeling confused and torn. When we pit them against their other family, we're using them as emotional hostages.

We take unfair advantage of our children when we force them to take sides in family war games. What we're really doing is forcing on them the storm of feelings, the hurt, rage, and jealousy that we ourselves feel. Not only does this increase their distress, it deprives them of access to their *own* feelings. Most of us don't do this knowingly or with ill intent toward our kids, but our inability to resolve emotional issues creates additional trauma for our children.

In her recent book, *Second Chances: Men, Women & Children a Decade After Divorce,* Judith Wallerstein enumerates the difficult psychological tasks that children of divorce must perform in order to adjust successfully to their parents' divorce. They must: understand the divorce; deal with the loss of one parent from the permanent household; work through their anger and their guilt; accept the permanence of divorce; remove the divorce from the center of their thoughts so that they can get back to their own lives. And, finally, they must learn to believe that they are still entitled to lasting, loving relationships. With all these complex adjustments to make, not to mention learning to live with a new second family, our children have their emotional work cut out for them. It is certainly our responsibility as parents to do all we can to prevent their having to act out *our* negative feelings for us—thereby making their burden that much heavier to bear.

Second-wife Roseanne is in a stalemate with her wife-in-law, Jan, who had been her friend before Roseanne began a relationship with their mutual husband.

> I understand my wife-in-law's anger, but it's a shame that her three-year-old son has to suffer as a consequence. Whenever my husband and I go to pick Alex up for the weekend, she's waiting for us inside by the window. As soon as she spots our car, she just shoves little Alex outside. There he is by himself on the front steps, confused and upset. She never comes out, and Alex is always reluctant to come with us. It's heartbreaking.
>
> I want to talk things over with Jan, but I know she doesn't want anything to do with me. I feel guilty about the whole thing too, because now Alex mistrusts his own dad and me. I just want to find a way we can all work this out so that Alex can become part of our family and get his dad back.

One solution for Roseanne might be to ask her husband to talk to his ex-wife. He is undoubtedly disturbed by his son's fear and withdrawal also, and eager to break a stalemate that could cripple the little boy's emotional development. In opening a dialogue with his ex-wife, Roseanne's husband might begin to create an atmosphere of mutual understanding and civility, from which his son can benefit immeasurably.

On the other hand, Roseanne may be letting her own negative assumptions about Jan prevent a possible dialogue between them. Such assumptions thwart open communication, which is always worth exploring in these hostile, damaging situations. Talking to Jan certainly couldn't make things worse. If face-to-face contact is too intimidating, Roseanne might try writing her a brief note to the effect that she's concerned about Jan's feelings, she's concerned about Alex, and she's concerned about her own family. What can they all do to improve the situation for everyone involved? Jan may fail to respond positively, but Roseanne will at least know that she did her best to try to resolve a crucial problem.

Children from former marriages often walk a difficult road. They not only have to deal with their mother's bitterness toward the new stepfamily; they must also relate to a stepmother and stepsiblings who may not be ready or willing to accept them. When the mutual husband/father fails to help his child through this painful adjustment, the youngster is left to devise her own coping strategies. A child might try to avoid spending time with her father's new family. Or, when she is with them, she might play out her confused feelings by being petulant or derisive or withdrawn. It's worth remarking that there's often very little difference between the behavior of a two-year-old and that of an eighteen-year-old in these circumstances. The emotions are raw, the agony close to the surface, and a hurt, confused teenager often has a lot in common with a bewildered toddler. The bottom line is that neither wants to accept the cold, final reality that the family is now split in two.

In cases such as these, former wives must take it upon themselves to talk with their ex-husbands about the difficulty their child is having adjusting to the stepmother and/or the new family. The mutual husband/father should, first of all, make an extra effort to assure his child that he still loves him or her. He must also explain to the child that the stepmother is new to the family and that it will take time before everyone feels comfortable, but that things *will* get better. It's especially important for the adults involved to be candid with children of all ages. Don't paint a rosier picture than actually exists, thus denying the child's own valid perceptions. Acknowledge that problems exist, but assure children that all members of this changed and changing family want to work together to make life easier and happier. And finally, *listen* to your children. Let them know that it's okay to express their feelings—even if those feelings reflect negatively on one or more parents or stepparents. If you know how your child is experiencing a troubling situation, you can address his conflicts more directly.

Defaulting on our responsibilities as parents and stepparents can deprive our children of the love and guidance they need and deserve. Former-wife Denise talked about her son's difficult confrontations with his father's second family.

When my husband and I got divorced, David was only seven. In the beginning, my husband was very involved with him. In addition to his regular visits, he was active in David's Scouting programs and always made sure to attend every one of his soccer games, even though he had to drive an hour each way. When he remarried eight years ago, things really began to deteriorate—primarily due to my wife-in-law's alcoholism, which she didn't acknowledge. Whenever she had a crisis, she'd make David the scapegoat. She was unable to deal with her own kids or herself, so it was easier to pin it all on him. Needless to say, it didn't take long before David began to dread his visits to his dad and his stepfamily.

My ex-husband, who had been the model divorced father, sided with his second wife in an attempt to preserve their marriage. They were getting counseling and were told to have minimal contact with us, which soon became no contact at all. Something was definitely wrong with that counselor; I don't see how anyone could recommend that a father not see his own son. In any case, David's contact with his father has indeed been minimal since then—and that was about two years ago. David's almost a teenager now and really needs his father. It seems grossly unfair that he should have to wait until his stepmother gets her life together.

When parents are ill-prepared or don't take the time to help their children through the difficult transitions brought about by divorce and remarriage, the unhappy consequences can be far-reaching. If a child doesn't get a chance to express and work through his feelings about the upheaval in his family, he may have trouble in relating not only to his parents and siblings but to friends, teachers, and others. He may start having difficulty in school or may withdraw from activities he once enjoyed. Teenagers may become sexually promiscuous or begin toying with drugs. Older children of divorce—even those in their twenties and thirties—may have a hard time developing or sustaining a healthy relationship with the opposite sex.

When serious problems go unaddressed and unresolved, they become manifest in people's behavior and sometimes in their physical health. One ten-year-old child whose parents had divorced and both remarried within several years developed a stomach ulcer. Both his mom and dad had assumed that he had successfully adjusted to the family changes because he seemed outwardly content. But his body told another story. Again, parents must help their children understand why the divorce happened, help them accept the consequences, and yet encourage them to have a positive outlook about relationships in general.

Often professional help is required, but that shouldn't take the place of a parent's love and concern. Children need to know not only that their parents still love them but that what happened to their parents won't necessarily happen to them. They need to have faith that they can forge trustworthy, lasting relationships, even though their parents' union ultimately failed.

Current-wife Nadine found herself trying to overcompensate for what she saw as her wife-in-law's neglect of her teenage daughter, Nadine's stepdaughter. The girl's problems adjusting to her father's remarriage affected every member of both families.

> I'm a strong advocate of professional counseling, but I resent spending about half my therapy time talking about my wife-in-law and my stepdaughter. I feel sorry for the girl, because I think she's been hurt by her parents' divorce. But taking the extra time to deal with her emotional problems is a burden I feel I shouldn't be faced with. I want to be a good stepmother, but I don't think I should have to replace her real mother. While my wife-in-law is off on dates or taking trips with her girlfriends, my husband and I are left to take up the slack. I think I'm entitled to time alone with my husband and our own daughter without feeling guilty about excluding my stepdaughter from certain outings or vacations. I waited twenty-eight years to have a child, and now I want to give her the best possible life I can without feeling guilty that my stepdaughter is somehow being cheated.

Adolescence is a difficult period for most children, but for children of divorce it is particularly fragile. They're looking forward to that time in their life when they'll be getting involved with the opposite sex, yet their own family experience is one fraught with betrayal, disillusionment, and impermanence. Had Nadine's husband and wife-in-law devoted the necessary time and attention to their daughter when the divorce first occurred, she might not have experienced such wrenching emotions when her father remarried. But it's never too late to begin to come to terms with troubling emotional issues. Perhaps Nadine should allow her husband the time to be alone with his daughter on occasion. Even a couple of hours a weekend together might enable father and daughter to work through some of the feelings that continue to plague the young girl. Quite often teenagers also benefit from peer support groups, and many now exist for children of dysfunctional families. Nadine might want to suggest this option to her stepdaughter, or have the girl's father or mother approach the subject. Having the opportunity to discuss family problems with other teenagers from similar backgrounds could prove helpful and healing for this young girl.

While Nadine has every right to feel that she and her own daughter are currently getting the short end of the stick, the situation will not improve by her getting riled over her wife-in-law's cavalier behavior. The sooner her stepdaughter's problems are addressed and confronted, the sooner everyone in the family can begin to lead a normal life.

Whose Side Are You On?

Children are entitled to the love and support of their parents, and their need may be greatest during the emotional upheavals of divorce and remarriage. Kids shouldn't have to deal with these adjustments on their own. However, when we are in the midst of our own emotional storms, it's sometimes difficult to put their interests first when we ourselves are so needy. Even though we may desperately need a shoulder to cry on, we must not make our children play the role of our parents. We need to be careful that we don't, consciously or unconsciously, assign our child the role of caretaker or go-between.

Reverse parenting occurs when we expect our child to take care of our needs. If we demand that our children show their loyalty to us by withholding love or affection from their other family, we put them in a double bind: If they love someone we disapprove of, they risk losing our love; yet if they are "loyal" to us, they have to shut down their own feelings. Maneuvering in this no-win situation, children risk damaging their own emotional development.

Current-wife Gabrielle talked about how her three step-daughters withdrew any allegiance to her as a way of protecting their own mother.

I had known my stepdaughters for years before I became their father's wife and their stepmother. I had been their swim instructor and baby-sitter, and they knew and liked me. But when I became their stepmother, they didn't want to like me anymore. It was terribly confusing for them. They obviously held me responsible for their parents' split-up, even though it was actually their mom who wanted the divorce.

The girls were seven, eleven, and fifteen when I married their dad. We'd do things together, go shopping and to the movies, but as soon as they started having a good time, they'd feel guilty and turn on me. I asked them kiddingly, one time, what was happening, if they had huddled and decided they had to "get" me. "Yeah, something like that," they said. Over the years when the girls would come to visit, it was always a mixed thing. I had a sense that they were really happy to come, and yet they held themselves in check. When their mother broke up with her boyfriend, they resented me even more, because she was so unhappy. They couldn't allow themselves to enjoy their time with me. It was so sad—no one ever gave them permission on the other side to have a good time on this side.

Do we inadvertently force our children to take sides? Does the wife-in-law relationship necessarily consist of opposing parties? When I spoke to the women in this study, most of them admitted that communication with their wives-in-law was difficult because they basically distrusted or disliked one another. Not surprisingly, over half the women reported that direct communication was infrequent; another third said they never communicated directly with their wives-in-law. What communication there was frequently occurred via the children. Indeed, three quarters of the ex-wives said they had learned virtually everything they knew about the current wife from their children.

When children are assigned the role of messenger, interpreter, or censor, what effect does it have on them? Many learn to edit their thoughts before they speak in an effort to appease both households and protect themselves from recrimination. Talking thus becomes a risky business, and some children just clam up. Former-wife Beatrice told me how her children gradually became "double agents," adept at withholding information from both households.

> Mia and Ben are six and nine. They're very close both to my ex-husband and me—and I think they're becoming quite fond of both their stepmother and their stepfather. But neither of them seems comfortable talking about their stepparents—especially in a positive light. I think they think it would upset me to hear that they had a good time with my wife-in-law, as if we were somehow in competition. On the other side of the fence, my ex-husband used to ask them so many questions about my new husband that now they refuse to talk about him at all. They just change the subject when it's brought up. It's like one household doesn't exist for them when they're in the other one. They got real good at just being quiet.

Even when former wives and ex-husbands have come to terms with their breakup, sorted out what happened and why, and explained it all to their kids, the children may still feel a lot of confusion and anger. It often seems to young children that their parents have conspired against them, punished them for being bad by breaking up. And if either parent then remarries and has additional kids, that makes things even worse, since there are now "outsiders" vying for their parents' love.

As parents and stepparents, the most important thing to remember is to communicate with your children, let them know you're there to listen to their concerns, and remind them that you love them and want them to feel comfortable with their new family. If problems persist, family counseling is an excellent way to work with your kids on overcoming conflicts surrounding divorce, remarriage, and adjustment to family changes. We'll talk more about the role of counseling in the last two chapters.

Among the most stressful times for children of divorce are those occasions when both families must come together—family celebrations, school events, graduations, and weddings. In the midst of what should be joyful milestones, they're preoccupied with concerns about how their divorced parents, stepparents, and extended family members are conducting themselves. The children, who should be the happy stars of these special occasions, are left to worry about which of their relatives is feeling awkward or anxious. Often, they try to avoid conflict between their parents by taking matters into their own hands, attempting to identify and resolve problems before they erupt.

One current wife told me that her five-year-old stepson advised her that she was to sit in the last row at the Christmas play so that his teachers wouldn't mistake her for his mother. Another worried student begged her mom to let her stay home from her junior-high graduation so that she wouldn't have to face seeing her stepmother and mother together. "It's awkward all the way around," said one first wife, the mother of two. "My daughter is already—a whole year ahead of her college graduation—worried about how she is going to handle the event with all of us there."

Current-wife Grace has realized for some time that there would be events in her stepson's life at which she would be called upon to show up and be civil and gracious. Although she had, on occasion, been in the same room with her wife-in-law, their first public appearance together was at her stepson's high-school graduation. What Grace didn't anticipate was how her stepson would react to the meeting.

> We all wanted to embrace Bobby, congratulate him, and fawn all over him, as he has been fawned over all his life by two separate sets of parents. But we had never all been in the same room at the same time. After the ceremony, the four of us descended upon him and started to congratulate him, and he ran the other way. He spent the entire afternoon with his girlfriend and her parents. Well, this made it even more imperative that the four of us get along, since we couldn't rely on Bobby to cut the ice. We talked about him, kept him as the focus of the conversation, and everybody was on their absolute best behavior.
>
> As the afternoon progressed and we all realized we could be civil to one another without any terrible consequences, Bobby's real parents—my husband and his ex-wife—began to criticize him. They were hurt and insulted that their son had decided to spend such an important occasion with his girlfriend rather than with them. But I think Bobby made the right decision. He had a place to go that was neutral and where he didn't have to be in the middle of things. We all felt pretty stressed out that afternoon, so I imagine he would have felt even worse had he been with us.

Acting Like Grown-ups

One wonders if Bobby would have felt so uncomfortable had both his families sat down with him before the graduation and asked him how he was feeling about the upcoming event. This would have allowed him to express his feelings of anxiety and nervousness while giving both sets of parents the opportunity to assure him that they would do everything they could to make him feel comfortable. As awkward as these meetings are, facing them often turns out to be less stressful than endlessly avoiding them. At some point we have to begin to take responsibility for the changes in our lives by dealing with them head-on. That doesn't mean putting a happy face on everything all the time; it does mean giving our kids a fair chance at a happy life. Our split households are not their responsibility, and it's unfair to require them to pick up the pieces. Doing what we can to meet our wives-in-law halfway not only helps our children feel like members of two connected households but helps us feel more connected to our own lives.

Shortly after she learned of her ex-husband's upcoming marriage, Rachel faced the first "Parents' Weekend" at her son's university, an event they all (Rachel, her ex-husband, and his fiancée) planned to attend.

> The plan was that I would attend the Friday-evening activities and my ex-husband and future wife-in-law would arrive on Saturday in time for a parade, luncheon, and football game. I planned to leave after lunch, effecting more or less a "changing of the guard." The arrangements for Saturday lunch were still up for grabs. My ex-husband suggested that I attend one lunch function while he and his fiancée went to another, an arrangement which would have meant that my son would have to choose which parent to have lunch with. I picked up the phone and called my future wife-in-law and suggested we all have lunch together. "I think we have a lot of awkward times to get over," I told her, "but we're going to be sharing a lot of important occasions in the future. We've got graduations and weddings and christenings where we'll probably be together, and it would be nice if we could get beyond this stiltedness and learn how to be comfortable with each other. The main thing is that I don't want our son to have to make a choice about whom he's going to spend time with."

She and my ex-husband agreed, and the lunch went pretty smoothly. It just took someone making that first step. My wife-in-law didn't feel quite as relaxed that afternoon as I did, but over the years we've come to accept one another.

In addition to paving the way for a smoother relationship between herself and her future wife-in-law, Rachel did her son a great favor by overcoming temporary embarrassment in order to bring everyone together. She overlooked whatever resentment or antipathy she might have felt for her ex-husband or his fiancée in favor of coming together as a family—a family separated by divorce, but a family nonetheless.

When divorced parents work out difficulties between themselves—and it's never too late to do so—children, regardless of how old they are, feel better about their families and themselves. Even adult children of divorce suffer from having to mediate between their parents—or between their mother and stepmother, as in Beatrice's case.

Beatrice found herself caught in the middle, having to contend with the tension between another generation of wives-in-law, namely, her mother and stepmother. The occasion was her own second wedding, and luckily the event provided an unexpected opportunity for the senior wives-in-law to break the ice.

My parents' divorce and my father's remarriage took place only a few years before I decided to remarry. It was a sticky situation that had resulted in a lot of bitterness on my mother's part and a lot of pettiness on my stepmother's. Until my wedding, in fact, they had taken pains to avoid each other. So I went to a lot of trouble planning my wedding and all the events prior to it so that they wouldn't have to see each other. I engineered all kinds of ways to keep them apart. I even gave each of them a chart specifying which side of the room was their "turf" at the reception. But when we cut the cake and my dad gave the toast, they somehow bumped into each other—and ended up talking to each other for about forty-five minutes. The guests at the wedding were abuzz. Here were the two rivals chatting each other up! Since then, I've had them together for many family occasions, and they get along fine. I can't tell you how happy it made me that the last time they were together they seemed to genuinely enjoy each other's company.

When we make an attempt to get along, or at least to be more civil with our wives-in-law and ex-husbands, it not only makes our children feel more secure, it also provides them with models for healthy adult relationships. On the other hand, when we constantly berate our children's "other set" of parents, they come away with little experience in how to relate positively to people. Similarly, unless a child is given some sense that a man and a woman can be happy and loving together, he won't know how to have a good, loving relationship himself. Wallerstein's *Second Chances* convincingly documents how children carry the scars of divorce with them into adulthood, often making it difficult for them to forge lasting relationships with the opposite sex.

Even when a former wife finds it impossible, in spite of all her efforts, to maintain a decent relationship with her ex-husband, she can make sure her children are aware of her good memories and happier feelings of the past. And she can point to her own current relationship or marriage as a positive model.

Current wives, too, can do their part to reinforce this. When we show our kids that we can be kind—or at least pleasant and civil—toward their "other" parents, we're giving them an invaluable gift. Moreover, we ourselves benefit by letting go of our bitterness and anger—stressful and destructive emotions to carry around year after year.

If kids of divorced parents had their choice, most would

undoubtedly opt for their mom and dad getting back together again. Recent studies have shown that even adult children of divorce find it difficult to give up the fantasy that their parents will one day reunite. Since we cannot change our lives to accommodate our children's fantasies, we can at least learn to approach our family and wife-in-law relationships with enough openness and respect to help assure ourselves and our children happier lives.

Custody: Who Gets the Friends? Who Keeps the In-Laws?

*Can Friends Be Friendly with Both You
and Your Wife-in-Law?*

I was a wreck after André and I split up. Here I had waited until I was thirty-seven to get married, had finally thought I had made the right choice . . . well, obviously, I was wrong. When I began to put my life back together again, I was glad that at least I had my friends—they had always been there for me through everything else. Boy, was I in for a rude awakening! André had gotten to them already, had cried on their shoulders about how hard the marriage had been on him, blah, blah, blah. So I begrudgingly accepted the fact that we'd be sharing my old group of friends. That was, until Babs came along. He married her after only six months of dating her, and now *she's* hanging out with my oldest, dearest friends. I still see some of them on a one-to-one basis, but I'll never feel comfortable being in a group with her and my ex.

Linda (ex-wife)

Probably the most unanticipated rivalry wives-in-law experience is over the issue of friends. We expect to do battle over child custody, property settlements, alimony. But parceling out our good friends can be almost as difficult. Must friends be dragged into the emotional tug-of-war created by divorce and remarriage? Is it their obligation to take sides or to refrain from doing so? In Linda's case, she was able to maintain individual friendships but no longer felt comfortable as part of the old crowd. Not that her friends didn't want her to be part of their social life—in fact she continued to receive invitations to dinner parties and holiday functions. But she had to be willing to accept the fact that her ex and his new wife might be there too, and that meant a stressful occasion that she knew she wouldn't enjoy.

Former and current wives struggle with similar dilemmas, seeking solutions they can live with. Current-wife Thelma talked about her early difficulties with her husband's old group of friends.

To this day I can't watch a football game without feeling like tackling my wife-in-law. My husband and I are both football addicts and planned to get all our friends together for a pregame brunch. Since our wedding had included only our immediate families, this was going to be the first chance for our close friends to meet one another. I had mostly single friends at that time, but my husband's friends were almost exclusively couples he and his ex had known for years. Well, to make a long, agonizing story short, my husband invited six couples. The men all came, but only one wife showed up! It turned out the women boycotted our party per my wife-in-law's instructions. She explicitly told each of them that if they socialized with me, they could forget their friendship with her. Their husbands used the excuse that "the women weren't into football," but I later learned that was far from the truth. I was so humiliated. Our party was divided into two camps: my husband's friends acting like they were at some kind of bachelor party, and my friends sitting around feeling very awkward. The whole spirit of the day was completely ruined.

Actually, Thelma's experience is somewhat unique; Linda's is much more typical. In most cases, it is the current wives who gain custody of the mutual husband's family and friends. More than 85 percent of the current wives in our research stated that the husband's friends are closer to them than to the ex-wives, and 83 percent of current wives claim title to the in-laws. More than 80 percent of all wives in our survey stated that they don't have friends in common with their wives-in-law.

Many factors affect the loyalties of friends: whether or not wives-in-law have lived in the area a long time; the circumstances surrounding the divorce and remarriage; the individual expectations and personalities of the people involved, etc. Most friendships aren't as binding as family ties; friends just aren't as obligated or as likely to remain loyal in the face of wife-in-law competition. Unless the divorce is an amiable one, most people find it uncomfortable to remain on friendly terms with both members of a divorced couple—or both wives-in-law. This doesn't bode well for former wives concerned about retaining friendships connected to their former marriage.

According to the wives-in-law in this research, mutual friends of the former couple were most likely to retain friendships with both partners when the exes refrained from bitter discussions of the past and concentrated instead on present doings. In other words, our friends, like our children, don't enjoy being torn between two people they care for. We put our friends in a difficult, awkward position when we constantly berate our ex and expect them to chime right in with equally nasty remarks. Of course, there are those instances when friends felt closer to one member of the couple before the breakup, and that preference naturally dictates whom they remain loyal to after the divorce. Then there are those who call themselves our friends but who get a perverse pleasure from informing each wife-in-law about the other. They position themselves as double agents providing rundowns on whom the ex-wife is dating, what the current wife has to say about the ex-wife, and how the mutual husband acts with his new wife. Those are among the "friends" we are likely to lose.

Former wives, grappling with their new status as single women, are often dropped by married friends once the divorce is final. Rachel had a particularly difficult time adjusting to the new treatment from her former friends once she became a divorcée.

> We were a very tight group. Most of us had known one another since college. We'd gone through the ups and downs of career moves, babies, buying homes, and marriage problems. We used to joke that we were like the group of people in *The Big Chill*—only we couldn't dance and cook at the same time. Well, everyone was so supportive during my initial separation from Bud that I remember feeling overwhelmingly grateful for such close friends. I was constantly receiving phone calls and spent many evenings out crying on a friend's shoulder or agonizing about whether or not to get divorced. Some friends even offered to research marriage counselors for us. But once I finally decided to go through with the divorce, I became an "untouchable."
>
> I remember the first big blow came on my birthday—which I shared with one of the guys in our group. We had always made it a tradition to throw a joint party. As it turned out, this was our fortieth—a biggie. When I called him to see about making plans, he hemmed and hawed and finally muttered something about feeling awkward because Bud was now engaged to my future wife-in-law, and how could we both come to the same party? I was shattered. It's true, I would have felt somewhat strange at a party with Bud's

fiancée, but I had already met her and was getting accustomed to the idea of Bud having a new wife. After all, it had been my decision to get out of the marriage. So I had just assumed my friends would adjust to our new status, just as Bud and I were trying to. Anyway, I was really looking forward to the party as a way to break the ice and feel close to my friends again. But there was no party, and I couldn't push it.

And then Labor Day rolled around. We'd always had a picnic with five close families down at the lake, and that year no one called to invite me. I heard through the grapevine that Bud was bringing his new bride, but that wouldn't have bothered me as much as it must have bothered my old friends to think about having me and my wife-in-law at the same party. So Bud's new wife got to be with my friends while my kids and I settled for a pretty lonely backyard barbecue.

I've pretty much given up on the old crowd, and it's really very sad. I'm still close with one woman from the group, and she feels my being excluded has a lot to do with posing a threat to the other wives now that I'm without a man. I can't buy that—not after all our years of friendship. Anyway, I'm making new friends now, mostly single people, some quite a few years younger than I. I guess these changes are all part of the adjustment I have to make—but I'm very hurt and disappointed in the people I always thought would be there for me no matter what.

One issue Rachel's story raises is that former wives who find themselves newly single *are* frequently seen as a threat by other wives—even when those women are close friends. In fact, there are often subliminal feelings between close friends of the opposite sex, so the sexual paranoia is quite understandable. From the former wife's perspective, it seems as if her friends are treating her as an alien, abandoning her rather than sympathizing with her predicament. What is her solution? Certainly she can attempt to make new single friends for whom the "mate paranoia" won't be an issue. Or, she can see her women friends separately from their husbands, to avoid the issue altogether. Neither solution seems entirely just or satisfactory, but a wife-in-law must frequently resort to compromise until everyone involved adjusts to her new status.

Is it inevitable that one or the other wife-in-law gets exclusive custody of the former couple's friends? Not necessarily. There are those friends who are deeply committed to both partners in a former couple and weather the awkwardness in order to maintain separate friendships.

The popular TV series "thirtysomething" highlighted such a situation when Nancy and Elliot separated and their close-knit circle of four or five friends managed to stay in touch with both of them, despite many moments of embarrassment and hurt feelings. Someone, for example, accidentally drops a bomb by mentioning Nancy's new boyfriend in front of Elliot, who had no idea Nancy had already begun to date. Another time, Nancy comes to Michael and Hope's house earlier than planned, only to find Elliot in the front yard chatting with Michael. Both Elliot and Nancy feel somewhat betrayed, even though their friends are simply trying to make room for both of them.

TV characters aren't the only ones willing to suffer through the hard times in order to keep up longstanding friendships. There were testimonials by women in this study about friends who turned out to be "beautiful people" capable of genuinely caring about and remaining loyal to both exes. Admittedly not typical, such stories should encourage the rest of us. Wilma's was one such story. Her experience with social relationships at church certainly speaks well for the compassionate understanding of her friends.

My husband, his ex-wife, and I have all been active members of our church for years. Their split-up was definitely traumatic, but several years had passed by the time I started dating Willie. Even though his ex started seeing someone too, there was still a great deal of strain between us in the beginning. But somehow, our friends in the congregation helped us both overcome our jealousy and fear by accepting us and our situation. No one gossiped behind our backs, everyone was dignified and friendly, and we were both invited to Christmas and other holiday functions. It really helped to know that the people we call our friends weren't choosing sides or making judgments.

If you're a former wife and you're still close to mutual friends of your ex-husband, count yourself among the fortunate few. If, on the other hand, your old friends have dropped you, or if you're a current wife having a hard time being accepted into the fold of the former couple's circle of friends, it is often a situation that must be accepted. There are things in life we cannot change, no matter how hard we try.

You Don't Have to Divorce Your In-laws

In spite of the in-law jokes that are the mainstay of stand-up comics, many of the women in this study were grateful to retain a relationship with their in-laws and saddened when they couldn't. My research indicates that in-laws usually transfer their loyalty to the current wife. While 83 percent of current wives felt the husband's family was closer to them, only 40 percent of ex-wives felt they could "claim" the former family.

Many ex-wives who lose their in-laws to their wives-in-law take it philosophically. They understand that whomever the mutual husband chooses as his mate usually becomes his parents' choice as well; there is an understandable realignment of loyalties. "I'm no longer their daughter-in-law," Emily says objectively. "My wife-in-law is now related to my ex-in-laws, and I'm not."

Nevertheless, just as many former wives had very positive

stories to tell about their continuing relationships with ex-parents-in-law. When things go well, our husband's family becomes our family, and we spend years developing and nurturing those ties. Problems with our spouse usually have nothing to do with our in-laws and needn't change the way we feel about them as relatives. If we enjoyed a good relationship with them prior to divorce and remarriage, it should be possible to continue it. Former-wife Carla contends that her ex-in-laws are closer to her now than ever before.

> I have a genuine fondness for my ex-mother- and father-in-law. I always looked forward to family gatherings at their house during holidays and was grateful for their friendship and affection. I think I actually talked to my mother-in-law as frequently, if not more often, as to my own mother. I felt very comfortable sharing my problems with her and listening to hers. We liked a lot of the same things, too—foreign films, classical music. She and my father-in-law were really torn apart by our divorce and the fact that their son was seeing another woman. My mother-in-law wrote me a long letter, almost apologizing to me on her son's behalf, but also pleading with me to remain friends with her.
>
> It's been hard. When my ex-husband remarried he wanted to cut back on his financial obligations to me. My wife-in-law encouraged him, I'm sure. She'd like to see me cut out of the picture altogether, but that wasn't what the courts decided. And what happened then was that my ex-mother-in-law intervened on my behalf—telling her son it was his obligation to see to it that I was well provided for. I certainly never asked her to go to bat for me, but now my ex-husband has asked his parents to sever their ties with me altogether, a move which hurts me deeply. My ex-mom-in-law and I still manage to see each other on

the sly. We enjoy regular clandestine visits—even
sneak out to the movies together—unbeknownst to my
ex-husband and wife-in-law.

In my judgment, it is unfair to require former wives to
relinquish previous ties—and this often includes sisters- and
brothers-in-law—just because the legal connection has been
severed. Yet, in a majority of cases, even when connections to
in-laws have been built on years of loyalty and trust, they are
eventually broken.

Nancy had been close friends and business partners with her
sister-in-law for eight years. After her divorce and her husband's
remarriage, however, her close friendship with her ex-sister-in-
law began to suffer.

Lynelle and I own a boutique together. Until recently,
we were also best friends. In fact, it was through her
that I met my ex-husband, her brother. She originally
fixed us up when she and I were still in art school. She
was so thrilled that I hit it off with her brother—and
ecstatic when we became sisters-in-law. When Gary
and I broke up, Lynelle felt very bad about it, but she
understood because I'd cried my heart out to her when
Gary and I started having problems. The divorce didn't
really affect our friendship that much until my wife-in-
law came on the scene.

Gary's new wife feels very competitive with me,
especially because I'm in business with her sister-in-
law. Lynelle would come into the shop and tell me
that my wife-in-law pumped her for information about
me—how much money I made, what kind of buying
trips I went on, what kind of guys I was dating. Then
I'd fight back and make some down-and-dirty digs
about this woman I barely knew, and Lynelle was
caught in the middle. So finally we just put a gag order
on the whole topic. But as a result, something has

changed between Lynelle and me. We used to feel that
we could talk about everything, and now we're completely cut off. My wife-in-law has made us more like
strangers than best friends.

There probably wasn't too much Nancy and Lynelle could
have done to prevent the rift in their friendship. They weren't
used to holding back from one another, and so it was natural for
both of them, as best friends, to want to express their feelings
about Nancy's new wife-in-law. However, they ignored one
obvious fact: Lynelle was still her brother's sister and therefore
felt a family allegiance to her new sister-in-law. Her friendship
with Nancy may take a turn for the better somewhere down the
line—though the odds are not strongly in their favor—but right
now they need time to adjust to their new status as friends *outside*
the family.

They're Still Your Kids' Grandparents

Not all ex-in-laws feel sympathetic toward former wives. Some
blame them for the breakup of the marriage. Others never got
along with the former wives in the first place and don't bemoan
their departure. And many simply feel torn in the presence of
an ex-sister- or daughter-in-law who no longer seems to have a
place in their lives.

Whatever the circumstances, grandchildren and grandparents still need each other; and where there are children, ex-in-
laws are as much a part of the former wife's family as they are
the mutual husband's. The important ties between kids and their
uncles, aunts, and grandparents don't end when parents divorce.
While ex-wives may harbor bitter feelings toward their former
husbands, they usually realize that punishing them by withholding the grandparents' access to the kids is cruel and unnecessary.
Children benefit from more love, not less, and it's up to all the
adults involved to ensure that their kids aren't deprived of their
fair share. It's hard enough for children to have to divide their

love between parents in two separate households. If they sense that their moms get uptight around their dad's parents and family, they'll feel even more torn and distressed. When former wives keep up some kind of relationship with their kids' grandparents, everyone feels more like a real family. Rena recounts her experience sharing the Christmas holidays with her ex-in-laws:

> We all felt pretty nervous about getting together that Christmas, but I went along with my ex-husband's wishes so that my son could be with his grandparents during his brief leave from overseas duty in the Navy. My ex-husband and wife-in-law made a special visit in November to ask me if I would consider having his parents for Christmas dinner. My ex and his wife had to go out of town that year, but they wanted to make sure the grandparents would get to see Jimmy. I agreed to include them in our holiday plans, even though it felt very strange having them in my home after all that had happened over the years. I always felt they resented me for wanting a divorce, especially since I've never remarried. I don't know what my ex-husband has told them, but I'm sure they can't understand why I would give up a wonderful husband to strike out on my own. Anyway, we kept the conversation pretty superficial that day, concentrated on Jimmy, and they were very pleasant, really. They seemed a little sad that we had all been out of touch for so long—and I guess I was too. It was nice to feel part of their family again.
>
> I know my friends thought the situation rather bizarre. But I bear no grudge against them, and I don't stay awake nights worrying about what my friends think. It all comes down to making it easier for Jimmy to be together with his family on Christmas. I know that meant a lot to him. And it actually made me feel

good to establish some contact with his grandparents after all these years of "hiding" from them.

There are as many versions of in-law stories as there are wives-in-law, and they run the gamut from family lost forever to unexpected bonus relationships. Some former wives agree to get together with ex-in-laws only on very special occasions like graduations or weddings. Others feel more relaxed about their ex-families and see them as much or as little as they did before, and treat them the same way. Still others work out their own unique arrangements. I even heard from one former wife who was shocked to find out that her own seventy-year-old mother was moving in with her ex-husband's new family! The mother adored her son-in-law and never forgave her daughter for ending the marriage.

Although wives-in-law don't usually welcome each other into the new arrangements, in some cases there are pleasant surprises. Former-wife Danielle found that her wife-in-law's parents turned out to be the grandparents her ex-in-laws never were.

Both my parents died before Petey was born, and my ex-in-laws never really spent that much time with their grandchildren. They liked to pose with them for family portraits, but they never had much patience for little kids. My wife-in-law's parents, on the other hand, adore my son. They take him places, baby-sit for him, and treat him as if he were their own grandchild.

Even after my wife-in-law had a baby, and they finally had a "real" grandson to dote over, they continued to be close to Petey. He calls them "Gramps" and "Grandma"—and has never once considered them anything but full-fledged grandparents. I know it's unusual, and I'm really grateful to them.

Whether your own relationship with your kids' grandparents is as warm as Danielle's or as icy as that of the rival families on "Dallas," the important thing is to preserve the "grandparent connection." Since children of divorce must face so many complicated burdens and challenges—single parents, combined families, divided households, separate-but-equal stepbrothers and stepsisters—the least we can do is make sure their relationship with their grandparents is as uncomplicated and comforting as possible.

Do My In-laws Prefer His Ex?

While former wives often lament the loss of ex-in-laws, current wives face having to prove themselves. They take it for granted that in-laws and others will compare them to ex-wives on everything from physical appearance to career status to who makes the best Jell-O molds. Current wives talked about feeling tentative with new in-laws at first, wondering if the ex-wife was still missed. Most felt, though, that no matter how trying or difficult the transition period had been, they eventually won over the new in-laws.

"When comparisons get too odious," says current-wife Beatrice, "I try to do something that is very typically me and that makes the silent statement 'No, I'm not my wife-in-law; I'm another person who is also very interesting, who is separate but equal,' and I basically try not to worry about things I can't change."

Unfortunately, we're not all as balanced and resourceful as Beatrice. And, without question, many current wives face an uphill, sometimes even hopeless, battle in the attempt to win over their husband's family. Stacey talked about her painful first experience meeting her new in-laws.

My husband is Italian and has a huge, extended family. Even though his parents disapproved of their son getting divorced, they were very kind and warm toward me from the beginning. I wish I could say the same for my sisters- and brothers-in-law, and all the aunts and uncles.

We had a huge reception after our small wedding, and I was so upset I almost ducked out after the first hour. Nearly everyone ignored me, except my mother- and father-in-law and the kids under age ten. The reception line was the worst. Most of my husband's family just glanced over at me as if to say, "Oh, so you're the new wife, huh?" Not one person came up to introduce themselves to me, so I spent the entire afternoon talking quietly to my own parents.

When it was all over and my husband and I were in our honeymoon suite, I burst into tears. I was sure we had made a mistake by getting married so soon after his divorce. I felt shut out, invisible. He was so sweet, assuring me people would love me once they got to know me better. Over the years, I've put a lot of effort into getting close to my new family—because family means a lot to me. I've become pretty good friends with two of my sisters-in-law since our kids play to-gether. They've confided in me that they had a hard time accepting me at first because they missed my wife-in-law and felt upset about losing her. I admit that made me feel kind of jealous, but I understood how they felt. The situation has improved a great deal, but I guess it just takes time for the family to get over the shock that my wife-in-law is gone and that I've arrived.

It's important for current wives to remember that it often takes time for in-laws to adjust to their son's or brother's remarriage. There's a great deal of pain and disappointment when a family member divorces, often sending shock waves through the entire family. A new marriage, however welcome, can be an additional shock because it's yet another change, and change, even for the better, inevitably brings stress. But if we can deal maturely with the necessary adaptations required of us, our reward will be a warmer, more comfortable connection to our new family.

The Ties That Bind

Family and friends often find the wife-in-law predicament—whom to be friends with, whom to stay loyal to—as bewildering as do wives-in-law themselves. Again, there are no rules of etiquette for them to follow in these matters. Those who've managed to sort out the difficulties and cut through the awkwardness are fortunate. Who gets defined as family is as much in the heart of the beholder as it is in the eyes of the law.

Charlotte's in-laws welcomed their son's ex-wife, current wife, stepchildren, and ex-in-laws with open arms to a big Thanksgiving dinner with all the trimmings. Of course they had the advantage of knowing that their son and his former and current wives—as well as all the kids—hadn't suffered the anguish of divided loyalties and therefore felt like family with one another.

> My mother-in-law is a trouper. That first Thanksgiving we all had together, she and my father-in-law ended up renting a banquet room at the community center because they didn't have enough space in their house for the combined families. My four kids from my previous marriage were there, as well as my wife-in-law's two from her marriage to my husband, and her baby from her present marriage. Then there were her parents, her husband's folks, my parents, my husband's two brothers and their kids, and several cousins! The next year we hosted Thanksgiving at our home, not worrying about the fact that the dinner had to spread out all over the house in order to accommodate everyone. Now we alternate between my mother-in-law, my wife-in-law, and myself. I think the key to all our "togetherness" is that my husband and his ex-wife had

a very amicable separation. They're still good friends, and she continues to be close to his mom. I like my wife-in-law a lot, too—and her husband is very down-home and easygoing. So there's really no underlying tension or strangeness there. Since we all feel pretty happy with the way things have turned out, our children and our parents seem to accept the added family members and take it all in stride. But it does make for a lot of dishes to wash up!

Most of us don't have "one big happy family." In many cases, even the attempt to blend everyone together might seem inappropriate. Obviously, when the divorce isn't a mutual decision—and most divorces are *not* amicable—one or both members of the former couple can be left feeling betrayed, rejected, angry, bitter. Until those feelings are resolved, wives-in-law usually confine themselves to separate camps, with family and friends being forced to choose between them. Many of us *do* eventually come to terms with the painful issues surrounding divorce and remarriage and go on to reestablish or develop close ties with those friends and family members who accept us for who *we* are—not whose wife we are.

Money—What We All Want

In the Good Old Days

Nowadays marriages are matters of the heart; divorces are largely matters of money. But it wasn't always that way. In Western Europe, until the late nineteenth century, marriage was primarily a financial arrangement between families. Economic exchange dictated the protocol that shaped conjugal unions: The marriage contract had little to do with compatibility or affection, and more to do with building stable financial alliances between families. Divorce was unheard of. The interested parties followed strict rules regarding a woman's dowry and the inheritance of the family estate.

The more traditional criteria of "marrying well into a good family" gave way to more romantic considerations when free courtship became an acceptable basis for marriage in the late nineteenth century. Yet, to this day, the marriage union very much implies financial obligations, and if we look closely, the shadow of earlier practices is still with us.

Our autonomous and self-sustaining nuclear families, not the extended families of the past, are now the primary economic unit. Financial survivability usually depends on two-income families; in the vast majority of marriages, husbands and wives are compelled to work in order to cover the escalating costs of living. We see less and less the old arrangement in which the wife works solely as a homemaker and the husband is the sole breadwinner.

Divorces, As Well As Marriages, Can Fail

Ballooning financial pressures and shrinking support systems drive the emotional and financial stakes high when a nuclear family divorces. We become painfully aware of this when we must confront the nasty business of divvying up the spoils of a failed marriage.

Good divorces involve reaching mutual understandings to divide and distribute worldly goods in ways that create fair, ongoing financial arrangements to the satisfaction of all parties involved. In bad divorces, both emotional and financial grapplings keep unresolved tensions bitterly alive so that the couple is inextricably bound. When there are no children involved, sorting out these details may be a matter of haggling about possessions and assets. But when child support and divided custody are at issue, a clean break is out of the question, especially when a second marriage has taken place and a new family is on the scene.

Money disputes pit current and ex-families against one another. Commonly, either too much money is going out or too little is coming in, the wrong person is writing the checks, funds are received too late. And rarely is there a "thank you."

Depending on whom you talk to, one family may see itself as the "have-nots" and the other as the "haves." At best, this view pushes divorced families back into court; at worst, it fuels family warfare. Battles over money become the ultimate source of power and control, the instrument of private agendas, fears, and ever-present emotional issues.

As I noted before, current wives are almost always in a

better financial position than ex-wives. The vast majority of ex-wives in this survey readily agree that their successors' lives appear more secure, while nearly as many current wives agree that the financial lives of their wives-in-law have worsened since the divorce.

Whether a woman does or doesn't have a husband or, even more directly, a marriage, often determines her financial status. In most cases, she enjoys a "promotion" if she is with a man and suffers a "demotion" without one. In this uncertain era, where the divorce rate is alarmingly high and the remarriage rate at an all-time low, hanging our entire economic security on whether or not we are wed may be risky business. The changing economics of marriage and divorce should prompt us to rethink traditional expectations about being taken care of financially.

I never gave the subject of money or where it was coming from much thought when I was married. In retrospect, if I had asked myself, *What could I contribute to our financial well-being if our economic situation were to change suddenly?* I would have saved myself a lot of time, fear, and nervous anxiety. But I didn't dare—mostly, ostrichlike, out of the naive belief that I would never have to. When I began my life as a divorcée, I had to face this chilling question—cold turkey!

Dependency: "My Divorce Gave Me My Last Chance to Grow Up."

Personally I feel somewhat exhausted from ten years of effort to recapture a lifestyle lost through my divorce, a struggle I might have avoided had I become more self-sufficient throughout the years of my marriage. Now that I have become financially independent, I've vowed never to surrender that hard-won independence again.

But, looking back, I understand the difficulties. I was determined to get a job, but raising my son alone placed tremendous stresses and strains on me in terms of establishing priorities and allocating my time. There were months on end when I doubted that I had the physical stamina or internal resources to manage it all. This was compounded by my many ambivalent feelings toward my ex-husband. I needed him when I didn't want to need him anymore. I was angry at him but couldn't risk letting that anger jeopardize the help he was giving me. I felt I was getting shortchanged while my wife-in-law was getting all the goodies.

Most of all I was afraid I would fail. For a time, I preferred trying only half-heartedly as a way of avoiding the risk of failure. So I was cutting myself off from any chance at the success that I eventually achieved. A friend of mine who plays the lottery gave me some good advice one day. She said, "If you don't play, you don't win." From the sidelines I took a long, hard look at my life and started playing.

Many women in this survey faced the same dilemmas I did when they became ex-wives. The first step, recognizing that many of us still feel dependent on men for security, is often the most difficult. Demmi has yet to overcome this major stumbling block. Her sense of entitlement is blocking her way toward self-sufficiency.

We were struggling from the first moment that we got married. Joel couldn't even afford an engagement ring, and although I said I didn't mind, I was still disappointed and somehow expected one. He had a lot of trouble keeping a steady job, yet he promised me that once we got married I would never have to work. But when things got tougher, he began insisting that I get a full-time job. I felt he was going back on his word, but started working part time as a compromise. The money I earned helped cover some of my personal expenses so he never had to spend a dime if I wanted a new lipstick or purse.

When Joel hit it big, careerwise, I quit my job because money was no longer an issue. You see, I made it possible for him to devote full attention to his career while we were married. Part of the reason we never had kids was so that we could spend time together. That way, I could pamper him when he came home at night. That was my job—he had his.

I left all the managing of major cash outlays up to him. He balanced the checkbook and took care of the big financial dealings like the mortgage and insurance. My marriage felt secure, like I was finally being taken care of—and I was, until the divorce.

I had lived through all my divorced friends' horror stories, so by the time my settlement came around I was scared to death I wasn't going to get anything. We'd been married five years, and when I did get a pitiful one thousand dollars a month, I was grateful. But my feeling now is that the amount falls woefully short of what I need to make it, and what Joel really owes me.

It's been four and a half years since our divorce and he's been making noises about his support coming to an end. When he remarried two years ago, I knew I had to play it cool so he wouldn't have an excuse to cut me off prematurely. But now the thought of being hung out to dry within the next year sends me into a terrible depression. Believe me, Joel won't get off the hook that easily. I'm seriously thinking of taking him back to court to see what kind of extension I can get. Since the divorce, I've had to start working part time again and my dad has helped with the loose ends. It seems to me that I put in my time with Joel and I shouldn't have to struggle like this. I shouldn't have to ask him to stick to his promise. After all, we made a deal while we were married and that's all there is to it!

No one should have to struggle, but many of us do. Promises shouldn't be broken, but many of them are. There is no question that too few women have ended up with a fair divorce settlement, and far too many have had to fight for what is rightfully theirs. But Demmi sounds more like a spoiled child than a disenfranchised marriage partner; unfortunately, petulant demands can't restore broken promises or heal wounded pride and are, in the long run, ineffectual. In today's divorce courts, Demmi's argument that her ex-husband "owes" her more alimony, without any indication that she has made a commitment toward self-sufficiency, would, most assuredly, fall on unsympathetic ears. More poignantly, beneath the bravado, Demmi is mourning an even greater loss: her comfortable, but ultimately crippling, financial dependency on her ex-husband and her former marriage.

Although most women suffer a sharp decline in their standard of living when they divorce, even when they have attained some measure of self-sufficiency, an alternative does exist. When both spouses acknowledge that they are contributing partners building an interdependency in marriage, their marriage is likely to be healthier and—if they join the unhappy statistics—so will their divorce. In that the partners have shared responsibility, each is in a better position to assume it on his or her own if the time comes. Women who are financially self-sufficient certainly don't escape the fears and trials of divorce, but it's much easier to get on one's feet and move ahead if one already knows how to walk. Alexis's scenario is strikingly different from Demmi's in this regard.

> Several years into my marriage I started to piddle around with some classes in marketing and sales because I thought that I might like to go into real estate when the twins were grown up. I didn't have anything specific in mind when I asked Drew if I could try my wings by working part time in his business. He was delighted and apprenticed me to the person in charge of coordinating all the company's sales presentations. At first I worked two days a week, kind of on a lark. I

still had a lot of responsibility at home and I had no intention then of working full time.

About a year and a half into my trial run, Drew's business, I mean our business, ran into some real problems. A major account dropped us for a bigger firm, and Drew was faced with layoffs. We put our heads together and thought that if I took the sales coordinating position, we'd save some money in salaries. I did it kicking and screaming but I had no choice at that point: It was help out or go under.

After three years, our business was starting to turn around, but our marriage took a dive. I blamed the work and pressure for our breakup and still have regrets that we put more into saving our business than saving our marriage. At first I was terrified I couldn't make it on my own, but it struck me that I had just been through a trial by fire, and I could finally afford to believe that I had what it takes to avoid catastrophe. If nothing else, I could take care of myself financially.

When it came to dividing our assets, neither of us had a single doubt that it would be half-and-half. Both of us had carried our weight and knew that splitting up was going to make money even scarcer. So we decided that I would spin off my own business. It made good survival sense for both of us emotionally and financially.

I have always been thankful that Drew encouraged my business talent and was smart enough to know a good thing when he saw it! Discovering my own ability, and even more, my own courage, when we struggled to save the business made a big difference when I had to face the loss of my marriage. I think I am less bitter about what I've lost and more willing to see what I've gained. That's been a lifesaver in many ways.

Financial dependency isn't an issue only for ex-wives. Current wives experience the psychological and fiscal drain when husbands must juggle their incomes to meet their obligations to former marriages. For circumspect current wives, recognizing and avoiding the financial vulnerability of their wives-in-law can be an important lesson.

My wife-in-law is a bloodsucker when it comes to Tony's money. They've been divorced for about twelve years and have one daughter whom he has supported all the way through college. It's not like he short-changed my wife-in-law—he even paid alimony until she remarried six years ago. But when her marriage ended two years ago she came right to Tony. She was in a tight money bind and upset because she wanted to buy a house but didn't have quite enough for the down payment. She had gotten herself a job doing secretarial work during her last marriage; her second husband never did have much money. After dropping about a thousand hints, the poor thing got around to asking Guess Who for fifteen thousand dollars. She made it sound like it would be a good investment, but I don't buy that! About the same time, Tony and I were talking about doing major kitchen remodeling and when her demand came in, Tony started saying that we couldn't do both. Like there was even a choice!

I couldn't believe that I would have to sacrifice what we planned just because she hadn't been able to get her act together, moneywise. I told Tony that he had to stop buying off his guilt and draw a final line. After a lengthy discussion, they came up with some kind of compromise that was infinitely more realistic, and I got my kitchen.

Believe it or not, some good things came out of this. First of all, Tony needed to cut that cord, and he's still working on it. Tony's ex is adjusting, slowly but surely, to the idea that she can't lean on him as much. As for me, I took a look at my husband's ex-wife and a little voice whispered, "Don't let that happen to you." Just because I'm married and things are good now, it doesn't mean that I can ignore my own life and let him take care of me. So I've started to rethink my voluntary retirement from paralegal work and realize that I should be maintaining my contacts so they don't just evaporate if and when I go back to earning a living. It would be disastrous to begin again professionally at square one.

Celia (current wife)

Celia's story is a good example of what happens when there are intergenerational as well as interpersonal issues between wives-in-law. When a man marries a woman who is a generation or so younger than his first wife, the significant age difference will almost invariably cause the women to see the world in different ways. Ideas about a husband's obligations in marriage and divorce fall right into the generation gap. Celia, a current and younger wife, hails from a generation steeped in the ideology and rhetoric of the feminist movement, with its commitment to independence and equality, whether a woman is married or not. Even if Celia doesn't fully practice these principles in her own life, they have a familiar ring and make sense to her.

Celia's wife-in-law, fifteen years older, was raised with a different set of expectations about her husband's obligations. From her generation's perspective, home and hearth have first priority and wives are expected to rely on their husbands, and even ex-husbands, as mainstays. The way her wife-in-law's life looks at the moment, "women's liberation" may mean something closer to "women's liability." The road back to financial solvency is steep and forbidding.

Such women are often training for employment for the first time in their lives, in a job market that clearly discriminates against age. They are competing for entry-level positions that pay significantly lower wages than those earned by co-workers who have devoted many more years to establishing seniority. It is understandable that, confronted with these harsh realities, a woman might seek help from the person to whom she entrusted her life in the first place—her ex-husband.

Most of the ex-wives I spoke with were hardworking and struggling to keep their heads above water. Typically they had scaled back their lifestyles after their divorce. They cut corners by moving into more-modest apartments, eating more dinners at home, and pumping their own gas. Even more importantly, they had scaled back their expectations and had aimed at more realistic appraisals of what were necessities and what were not. Most agreed that the deadliest trap a divorced woman could fall into was continuing to compare the financial advantages of married life to the belt-tightening times following divorce. Alida told of her experience.

> Whenever I was in a funk about money, I'd start beating myself up with the "What If" game . . . "What If" I hadn't divorced Oliver? Or, "What If" I had fought harder for the house in the divorce settlement? I could spend hours coming up with all sorts of fantasies about how great things would have been, If . . . and driving myself into a deeper and deeper depression. I counted all the mistakes I had made and all the opportunities I had given away.
>
> Not only did I never come up with any answers, but I wasted an incredible amount of time hiding from what I really needed to be doing: finding a way to make the life I now had more livable.

If you catch yourself playing the "What If" game like Alida, ask yourself another question instead: "What did I do today to make today better?" If the answer is, "More than yesterday," then you're winning!

Financial Obligation: The Root of Well-being or Resentment

Once couples live through the distribution of property—the home and its contents, the pets, the cars, the stocks, bonds, pensions, life and health insurance policies, and jointly owned businesses—there is often little energy and much less money left to make good on their financial obligations.

When the court dictates the terms of a settlement, what began as an honorable obligation may come to be regarded as a loathsome liability. If resentments are high and emotions drained, it's likely that each side views the other as greedy and selfish, grasping for more than is required or already possessing more than is needed. Comparisons come thick and bitter. Ex-wives stake first claim for their children while second wives insist on rights of their own. Mira tells it from the ex-wife's perspective, Sydney from the current wife's. Mira sees trouble down the line.

My kids tell me that my wife-in-law is doing a number on my ex about how his financial obligation to us is bleeding them dry. She wants him to go back to court and get the settlement changed. Her prime piece of ammunition has to do with us having a lot more money than they do. She says that with my new husband's salary and mine, plus what I receive in child support, we are way ahead. That's simply not true.

Maybe she doesn't know that my ex lied to avoid paying me more child support in the first place. He tinkered with his tax documents and put a lot of assets into his brother's name while we were just starting to talk about divorce. The burn is that he supports her and her one kid in the style to which she has become accustomed. Believe me, she does not do without and she doesn't even work!

I have *earned* every penny I get. Not only am I the full-time mom and dad, but I pay for all my teenagers' "extras," like the car insurance, the orthodontics, the twenty dollars here and there when they run out of their allowance.

Our divorce settlement came down ten years ago, and since then the price of living has skyrocketed. She apparently hasn't needed to notice.

She should be grateful that *I've* never gone back to court to get the child support payments raised. Then she would really have something to complain about!

Mira (ex-wife)

I really have very strong feelings about women not being left destitute by divorce. I also have feelings about women standing on their own feet. My wife-in-law could have gone to work a lot sooner than she did. I think she was trying to punish Ralph. She didn't go to work for almost eight years, and now that she is working she has done very well. When I think of all the years she spent doing volunteer work without getting paid, my blood curdles.

Her life as a prima donna came out of our pocket. When things got tight for Ralph and me, she showed no mercy. Ralph paid every dime the decree required, on time, every time. I went back to work to take up some of the slack and every so often I'd get into a funk because I felt *I* was the one who was supporting her.

Sydney (current wife)

Not all financial obligations are treated as emotional ransom. A number of both current and ex-wives in this survey felt that their arrangements were dignified and satisfactory. The most successful divorce settlements were characterized as agreements which were neither coercive nor punitive, but:

- treated the realistic needs of each divorcing spouse with equal validity and respect
- attempted to meet both parties' interests with multiple options
- represented a fair and mutual assessment of the couple's joint holdings
- took into account the quality of the continuing relationship

Divorces made in heaven? Not quite, but as close as they can come! Caroline, a current wife, marvels at the quality of her wife-in-law's divorce settlement and the positive repercussions it's had on the workability of their relationship.

I'm a little embarrassed to say that both my wife-in-law and my husband, Alvin, are to be commended—they have a first-class divorce! They worked hard to arrive at a mutually acceptable outcome after years of bickering about the original divorce settlement. This took a series of meetings with a lawyer who specializes in divorce mediation, not litigation.

Resettling the child support issue was the most difficult. After several stormy sessions about who was responsible for what, the mediator got them thinking about goals instead of grudges. Both Alvin and Helen wanted to encourage their teenage kids to be as self-reliant as possible, so the mediator began a two-way process to find the best possible solution. After a lot of back and forth, Alvin and Helen agreed to a joint parenting plan which meant that Alvin paid the child support money directly to the kids. They were responsible for reimbursing their mother for expenses, clothes, and food first. Whatever was left went for fun, so they had an interest in keeping basic expenses down. Alvin was relieved to send them the money directly because it took Helen out of the loop. As for

Helen, she didn't have to wait for her check every month. Each side got something they wanted. Even me. Alvin's involvement with Helen is greatly diminished and we all feel a lot cleaner about the break.

I'm proud of their shared willingness to experiment with solutions. Seeing them both in action also gave me new respect for Helen. Now when we do speak, which is substantially less frequently than before, I don't feel that underlying tension of "What does she want now?" She is no longer the enemy.

As for Alvin, I've always respected his determination to live up to his part of the divorce bargain, especially after reading statistics about how most ex-wives get shafted. It's rough out there and I'm aware of the struggle myself. In my darker moments, I know that he'd treat me the same way if he and I ever divorced.

Expect the Unexpected

Even with the best intentions, the state of personal finances fluctuates, and it is impossible to cover all future eventualities once the divorce settlement has been carved in stone. In the cycle of divorce and remarriage many things change on both sides: the ability to provide ongoing support, levels of need, liabilities for debts, including bankruptcy, and financially and emotionally destructive litigation.

These uncontrollable factors take on a new punch if either wife-in-law has children. As parents, we feel responsible for creating the best future we can for our children, and in today's world the future seems more expensive than ever. When second or sometimes third sets of children are competing for the same security, even compatible wives-in-law, inflamed with guilt, fear, and uncertainty, sound the battle cry. For example, Mildred was panicked when she received notice that her ex was petitioning for child support modification. He insisted his income was

declining, while Mildred knew for a fact that he had just sold off
some stock and was planning to retire.

I felt like I was in the middle of a "bait and switch"
scam. Even though it looked as if my ex would be
losing his yearly salary, his overall income was the
same as it had always been. It took me about two
minutes to call my lawyer, and her subsequent court
argument took the teeth right out of his petition. I was
so sure of my position that I began to feel like Clint
Eastwood when he says, "Make my day!" This time I
didn't fool around, and it paid off. I wasn't as timid
about fighting back as I was when we were in the midst
of the divorce. Back then I was a basket case, and now
I am a lot more savvy and confident.

Nevertheless, any kind of litigation is a test of
nerves. I was on tenterhooks the whole time, snappy
with the kids, weepy with worry about how I was going
to make it on less, and angry that Milt was taking us
for a ride. I ended up nursing a raging case of colitis.
But I doubt that Milt will pull that one again. Now he
knows whom he is dealing with.

These financial tugs-of-war are representative of the most
vehement of wife-in-law complaints. Ongoing expenses such as
education, milestone events such as weddings, and once-and-
for-all arrangements such as inheritance are left ambiguous in
more divorce decrees than one would expect.

Maureen and Zina represent two opposite sides of the
education issue. Maureen's ex-husband is paying college expenses for his current wife's children from an earlier marriage
but not for the education of his own children. He has begged off
by saying that he had put his children through private school for
twelve years and now the ball is in Maureen's court. This has
caused untold jealousies which Maureen's children blame on the

new wife and their father. Maureen hardened when she explained.

> My ex has tried to bail out completely, but he isn't going to get away with it any longer. If I have to take him back to court, I will. He's saying that now that the kids are eighteen, they are on their own as far as college is concerned. This whole thing came out of the blue, without discussion or any kind of consideration for their feelings. If I had known before, I could have started saving more money for their basic college expenses—and a first-class lawyer! It's June now and the oldest is going to start his freshman year in the fall, so I've got to scramble and borrow some money so he doesn't lose a term. That puts us all in the lurch for no good reason. My kids feel as though they've been disowned by their own father and don't want to have anything to do with him. And I feel he doesn't deserve their love if he's that unreliable and selfish.

Zina's divorce settlement spelled out her ex-husband's total responsibility for her daughters' university tuition and dorm expenses. She feels that his commitment to their future gave her children back some of the security that the divorce had taken away.

> It's something the two girls certainly deserved. They worked hard to keep their academic standings high during our breakup, and now they are being rewarded. They also know that just because their dad isn't living in the same house anymore, he is still their father and won't let them down.

Remarriage often results in broods of children who are roughly the same age and ready to begin their college years close upon each other's heels. Faced with this enormous financial undertaking, parents and stepparents start tightening their belts and looking for fat to trim. Current-wife Sara's predicament is not unusual.

> Between my kid, my husband's two kids, and my wife-in-law's two stepkids, we have paid out more than fifty thousand dollars in college expenses this year alone, and the horror doesn't stop there. With my wife-in-law's youngest coming up the ranks and ready to start as a freshman next year, it could go as high as sixty-five thousand. Something has got to give somewhere.
>
> At first, I found myself hoping that my wife-in-law's daughter would blow the SATs just so she'd have to go to a local junior college for a year, at least until my son had finished university. But when that didn't happen and she got into a first-rate school, I knew I had to start worrying seriously. Marjorie's current husband has two kids in college, too, so he's in no position to chip in on her kid's tuition. That means that Glen, our mutual husband, has got to bear the brunt. We all had this huge summit meeting to discuss the situation. We're hoping to find a scholarship for Marjorie's boy. If we don't, we'll have to look into long-term loans, though I hate to saddle young people with huge debts.

But what if the scholarships and grants aren't won? What if the tuition and living expenses are way out of reach? Here are some suggestions that may help everyone involved:

- Be Open About Difficulties. Young people have radar when it comes to problems. Parents need to initiate frank discussions with them to clarify the financial picture and support limitations.
- Don't Play Favorites. Particular attention should be paid to distributing college fund cutbacks fairly, so that the

newest freshman isn't taking the full brunt of the money crunch.

- Form a Team. Listen to your children's ideas and explore alternative options with them, such as work/study programs or part-time college attendance.

Our children's weddings also represent major outlays of cash, and wedding bells can lead to wedding battles. Although they are joyous, one-time (we hope!) affairs, the enormous expense is rarely addressed in divorce settlements and can be another source of financial strain on the wife-in-law relationship. In fact, responsibility for the substantial costs of those weddings had not been arranged in advance by any of the women in this survey.

> When our only daughter, Sylvie, got married last year, it took a lot of negotiation with my ex-husband to pull off the kind of wedding we wanted for her. My wife-in-law wasn't willing to spend a dime. That meant that he and I had to conspire, and for the first time since our divorce, we were on the same side . . . a little bit of an unholy alliance, but okay since it was for a holy cause.
>
> We worked out a plan that involved scaling back the guest list to a more affordable size and holding the wedding in the backyard of a friend's home.
>
> When my wife-in-law started making noises about the number of prenuptial parties we had planned, my ex-husband's parents stepped in and threw the engagement party, and my parents paid for the rehearsal dinner.
>
> The whole series of events was absolutely magical in spite of all the trimming back we had to do. Everyone pulled together to make it happen that way. Strangely enough, it might never have worked out so

well if we hadn't had my wife-in-law breathing down our necks.

Thea (ex-wife)

Finally, insurance policies, wills, estates, pensions—no coin of the realm is left untouched in the wife-in-law financial arena. When you have any questions whatsoever about financial matters, I can't stress strongly enough that you consult an attorney who specializes in these matters. Bear in mind that family law is under the jurisdiction of state law and varies across the nation. Don't assume anything about your financial rights until you've checked with an expert. There are fifty slightly different versions, all open to various interpretations.

Brenda and Ida will need to consult experts should their concerns escalate to open confrontation: Brenda is bothered that her children will one day have to share the mutual husband's life insurance benefits with his first set of children. "I don't resent all the kids getting what they deserve," she said, "it's just that it seems unfair that her kids will get what he and I have worked hard to build together."

Ida and her ex never had kids together, yet their financial obligations to children from previous and subsequent marriages continue to be linked. Ida told me that her ex-husband had rewritten his will so that all five children—Darren, her son from an earlier marriage, his three children from his former marriage, and his daughter with his current wife—share equally in the inheritance. "The children are all very close," Ida assured me, "but I wonder how my wife-in-law will feel about Darren receiving part of that."

These women's fears, concerns, and wishes highlight what many of the women in my research felt with respect to their current and ex-husbands' inheritance. The law is clear with respect to wills and divorce, but, again, it varies from state to state. In no-fault states, such as California, a dissolution of marriage *automatically* revokes existing bequests to a former spouse and also removes a former spouse as executor under any will made before the dissolution of marriage. Furthermore, in California, if your former spouse wants to include his ex-wife in his will or wishes to appoint her executor of his estate, he must write a new will after the divorce specifying this arrangement. But no matter where you live, it is a matter of going through the appropriate legal channels to clarify or contest any will.

Some wills are ironclad, and the deceased seem to succeed at ruling from beyond the grave. In these cases, the bequests we receive may have little to do with what we *feel* we deserve, but they can be perfectly legal. On the other hand, many wills are fallible and the more ambiguous they are, the more they are open to contest. If this is your situation, hire yourself the best legal representation you can afford—if need be, on a contingency basis. Don't be afraid to fight if you have done your homework and are convinced you have a legitimate claim. But remember, the law doesn't always deal in justice, only in legalities.

The Mutual Husband

I think it's about time my ex-husband stopped hiding behind my wife-in-law's ballsy behavior. She plays the heavy, and then he gets to come off as Mister Clean. The fact is, whatever she's nervy enough to demand—whether it has to do with the kids or our financial arrangements—it's always something he masterminded behind the scenes.

Jessica (ex-wife)

Were it not for the mutual husband, there would be no wives-in-law. A crucial, yet sometimes passive figure in the wife-in-law triangle, his attitudes and behavior are instrumental in determining how wives-in-law get along. Insofar as it is possible, most mutual husbands prefer to keep their distance from the wife-in-law relationship, yet they are often the ones credited when wives-in-law become congenial.

What part does the mutual husband play in the dealings between wives-in-law? It usually depends on three things: what kind of relationship he had with the former wife, whether or not he has resolved his feelings for her, and what kind of relationship he has with his current wife. While there are numerous ways in which the divorce/remarriage scenario is played out, the mutual husband usually finds himself in one of the following situations:

- He feels guilty about having left his former wife and manifests it in one of three ways: by bending over backward to please her, by displaying hostility toward her, or by ignoring her as much as possible. He may use his current wife to express his own unresolved feelings by having her "act out" on his behalf.
- He still loves his former wife and, despite his remarriage, is unable to acknowledge that their relationship is finished. Again, he may use his current wife to get back at his former wife, or try to foster a close relationship between the two so that the latter will continue to play a role in his life.
- He is repeating with his current wife the same unhealthy emotional patterns that were characteristics of his former marriage. Actively or passively, he tries to pit the two women against each other.
- He understands why his first marriage didn't work out, has discussed it openly with his former wife, and they have been able to come to an agreement about how their postmarital relationship will work. He is open and honest with his current wife and doesn't use either woman as an emotional weapon against the other.

Regardless of the dynamics between the wives-in-law and their mutual husband, if he has children, he is usually deeply concerned about maintaining ties to them. He's also in the delicate position of having to pull off an emotional balancing act between two separate households. Like the wives-in-law themselves, and their children, friends, and families, the mutual husband usually feels deeply divided and often distressed at the torn fabric that can never be made whole.

The Absentee Mutual Husband

One way of coping with the pressures of relating to a current and ex-wife and the children shuttled between two households is simply to retreat. Many men, even in this era of changing sex roles and increased awareness of the importance of fathering, give over all matters having to do with children and family to "the women." In most cases, this type of mutual husband was fairly uninvolved in parenting responsibilities prior to divorce, and so he's simply continuing a pattern—only this time around his behavior affects two families instead of just one. Now two wives must take up the slack when he turns away from his parental obligations. Natalie's ex-husband is a case in point.

It suddenly dawned on me that I was actually sharing child custody with my wife-in-law rather than the father of my children. I must admit that he'd never taken a very active role with the kids when we were married, but I thought he'd want to make it up to them when we split up—especially since they needed him so much more. The kids talk about him all week long and can't wait to see him on the weekends. Each Friday evening I dutifully drop them off at their dad's home for their scheduled visits, only to discover on Sunday night that he's spent almost the entire weekend on the golf course, leaving them with my wife-in-law. She's got an eight-month-old baby herself and can't really get out that easily, but it shouldn't be her responsibility anyway.

She and I have discussed this (since he's usually still at the club when I pick up the kids) and we agree that he isn't living up to his responsibilities as a father. When I do manage to talk with him, he defends his time on the green as "his release." He says he's asked the kids if they want to come with him and they always say no.

I don't see how he can expect a seven- and ten-year-old to relish quietly staying put in a golf cart all day. And I think it's especially unfair that he expects my wife-in-law and me to work everything out between the two of us. He's more married to that golf game than he's ever been to either of us!

Sometimes a mutual husband's withdrawal has less to do with male sex roles than leftover resentment toward his former wife. If it was her decision to end the marriage, or if there is residual animosity between them, chances are he still feels betrayed or bitter. Sometimes, with courage and resolve, he can work these feelings out with her. Short-term counseling can be immensely helpful, too, in coming to terms with what went wrong in his last marriage. But some men succumb to what seems an easier out: They cut themselves off from any dealings with the ex-wife, leaving the current wife holding the ball. Current-wife Monica talked about how her husband appointed her emissary to communicate between their household and her wife-in-law's.

I know Ken has never forgiven his ex-wife for having affairs during their marriage. It wasn't even as if she was in love with any of them—she dropped the guy who supposedly was the cause of their divorce shortly after the decree came through. So I understand his unwillingness to have anything to do with her. But, unfortunately, that spills over to his relationship with his daughter. He puts me in charge of talking to my wife-in-law every time a problem comes up: what summer camp we ought to send her to, why she isn't eating well, why she doesn't seem to enjoy playing with my daughter. Part of it, I think, is that my stepdaughter looks quite a bit like her mother, so she's a constant reminder to Ken. I just wish he could be more settled about his ex-wife—otherwise she'll haunt him forever.

Especially hurtful to former wives is seeing their ex-husbands being model fathers with their current offspring or with stepchildren, while withdrawing from their children of the earlier marriage. There's a moving and powerful scene in the film *Parenthood* when, after asking his absentee-dad if he can come live with him and being told, "No, it wouldn't work out right now," the teenage son smashes everything in his father's office, including a framed portrait of his dad with his new wife and baby. Mutual husbands do tend to lavish more attention on their "new" children. Some rationalize by saying the younger children need them more. Others say that they've acquired parenting skills with their new family that they never had with their former one. John Lennon was one example: He devoted far more time to his "new" son, Sean, than he had given to his older son, Julian.

Former-wife Carla had tears in her eyes as she recounted the situation with her ex-husband and his new family.

My ex and his new wife have no children of their own, but I hear that he has been a wonderful father to *her* children. Meanwhile, he's allowed his relationship with his own child, our daughter, to disintegrate. At first we set up weekends when she was supposed to visit them, but he kept canceling and rescheduling. Sometimes they'd call and want her on a moment's notice, so she'd hop right over. The one time my daughter called her father and asked if she could visit he said no; he was going on a camp-out with his stepdaughter that weekend. I will probably never in my lifetime forgive him for disappointing her so. And yet my daughter continues to yearn for her father's attention.

What makes things worse is that my present husband has been hungry to parent her for the last twelve years. But she has consistently rejected him, preferring to cling to the hope that her real dad will soon have time for her.

Recently she's been hanging out with some very weird kids, and I'm worried that they're a bad influence on her. She's withdrawn from me a lot, won't talk to me about her problems, and seems to have little interest in school. When I called my ex to ask for help, he told me it was my problem, not to bother him. He even implied that she was acting this way because of the inadequate job I'd done as a parent! He's never been there for her, and he's not there for her now.

It's true that Carla's daughter would benefit profoundly from a good relationship with her father, but from the story Carla tells, he doesn't seem willing to provide that. As unjust and sad as the situation currently appears, there's no way Carla can compel her ex-husband to be a father to their child. What she *can* do is make certain she doesn't transfer the anger she feels toward her ex to her daughter. Her daughter needs help in understanding that *she* is not to blame for her father's withdrawal from the family. It would be helpful for Carla to explain to her daughter, candidly and calmly, that her father is simply not living up to their expectations. Carla's daughter has every right to feel hurt, cheated, angry. If she can express those feelings openly, perhaps she won't need to act out her suffering with her "weird" friends. Once she faces the reality that her dad is not the fantasy father she yearns for, perhaps she'll be more open to receiving affection and attention from her stepfather, who desperately wants to fill a paternal role for her.

Stirring Up Trouble

There are many reasons why mutual husbands, consciously or unconsciously, create friction between wives-in-law. In some instances, it may be another way to withdraw. If two women are embroiled in a hot-and-heavy cat fight, mutual husbands have a great excuse for not "getting involved." Others actually enjoy "watching the fireworks," as one wife-in-law put it, and feel flattered to be the cause of the sparks. Then there are the men who like to join in the fray, usually in order to unconsciously work out some unfinished emotional business. Randall was one such husband. His ex-wife Wendy explains.

I couldn't understand why I was always so ticked off at my wife-in-law. I had nothing against her, really. If anything, I felt sorry for her. She's suffering at the hands of the same person who emotionally abused me for so long. But now I realize he was goading her on. All her snide remarks to me had something to do with my being self-centered; whether it was my wanting to leave the kids there for a couple of extra hours, or my asking to reserve certain holiday times with my kids, she always accused me of never thinking of anyone but myself. It all started sounding vaguely familiar—those were all my ex-husband's old accusations. Whatever our problem, whenever I was standing up for myself, he'd always pin it on my "selfishness." Well, I continued to stand up for myself with my wife-in-law until finally my ex got involved and created a torrential argument over absolutely nothing. It all came back to me—all the reasons I couldn't stay married to him anymore. I guess she can handle him better than I did. But I still feel sorry for her—and I now know there's no arguing with either one of them. I just have to stand firm and hold my ground.

Sometimes "troublemaking" mutual husbands are forced to confront their behavior and straighten out their act when their current and ex-wives jointly refuse to serve as emotional mouthpieces. As with much hurtful and destructive behavior perpetrated against us, when we assert ourselves and refuse to be a party to it, we can usually avoid being the target. Peggy talked about her experience with her ex-husband.

I used to blame my wife-in-law for a lot of things that were really my ex-husband's fault. She was my "whipping boy," and it was easy for me to dump everything that bothered me about being divorced and having to share custody of my kids onto her.

One afternoon she came by to pick up the kids. They weren't ready to leave yet so she and I had a chance to really talk for the first time. She told me that my ex didn't want her to get to know me for fear we would gang up on him. She said she wouldn't have minded alternating weekends with the kids as I had suggested, but my ex had insisted she nix the plan. Things were still new with them, and she hadn't wanted to upset him, so she went along with his demands. But she was getting as weary of all the unnecessary hassles and conflicts as I was. So we made a pact to let him fight his own battles from then on.

The next time I called, she put him on the line rather than running interference as she always had. I was more flexible about working things out, which disarmed him somewhat, and we were able to reach a better compromise. Now, instead of watching from the sidelines while my wife-in-law and I tear each other's hair out, he's taking the knocks himself—which really means taking responsibility for his own part in family history, past and present.

Mediators, Comrades, Friends

Not all mutual husbands engage in emotional combat or encourage wives-in-law to do so. Nor do they always absent themselves from the responsibilities of dual households. Almost 10 percent of the women in this research described their mutual husbands as "mediators"—for the most part keeping wives-in-law apart by keeping former and current family affairs almost completely exclusive of one another. Some rarely, if ever, spoke to their current wives about specific dealings with ex-wives except when absolutely necessary or in the event of an emergency. Actually, a husband who never brings up the subject of his ex-wife can make a current wife just as uneasy as one who talks about her incessantly. It's normal for a current wife to wonder about her predecessor, and when there is a news blackout, it's even easier to fantasize feverishly about her.

"Mediating" mutual husbands try to protect both wives from hurt feelings and the traumas of double families. In the case of Shelly's husband, his well-meaning efforts almost backfired.

One of the reasons I fell in love with Tom was that he's such a decent, caring human being. But sometimes he's almost *too* nice; people tend to walk all over him. Last summer my wife-in-law got a grant to study in Europe, which meant there'd be no one to take care of my eight-year-old stepdaughter for two months. My husband took it upon himself, without even asking me, and simply made the arrangements for Tanya's daily activities on his own: She'd go to work with him in the mornings, play and do art projects in his office, and then he'd take her to day camp in the afternoon and pick her up at four-thirty. When he told me what he'd worked out, I was somewhat taken aback and hardly had time to respond before my wife-in-law called to find out why I didn't want Tanya around. I'm a teacher, so I have summers off, and I told her that I would have been happy to take care of Tanya part of the day, but Tom had never asked me. My wife-in-law and I both ended up angry with Tom, until we realized that he was only trying to do what he thought was in everyone's best interests. He didn't want to burden me with Tanya for the summer, but he didn't want my wife-in-law to curtail her study plans either. So he tried to please both of us—and Tanya—only to find himself cast as the villain in a subversive plot! Of course when I realized how caring his motives were, I stopped being mad, but I did suggest to him that we start learning how to function more like a team.

Being part of a team or a "united front" with their husbands was how many current wives described their interactions with wives-in-law and former families. Some don't want to get in the middle between their husband and his ex, for fear of jeopardizing their own marriage. Others don't really care to be involved at all but feel they must support their husband's decisions and attitudes regarding his former wife. But the primary reason for dealing reasonably with the ex-wife was to make things easier on the children. As Tina observed . . .

It's hard enough for kids to sort out what *two* parents feel or expect of them, not to mention two *divorced* parents and one or more stepparents. To make matters worse, we adults were treating each other like warring nations. Even though we all had to go through the self-hate and sabotage stages, we owed it to ourselves and our kids to bury the hatchet. Now I try to work together with my husband and his ex-wife to send a consistent message about whatever issue comes up. If we *don't*, our kids will play us against each other—play off the bitterness—and everybody loses.

Altruistic motivations aside, the mutual husband often goes along with whatever the current wife wants in order to keep peace at home. He may feel conflicted and torn, but if he's forced to "choose" between the former family and the current one, he usually opts for the family housed under his own roof. But he feels constantly embattled, trying to please all his family members at least some of the time. This creates tremendous pressure on him and, almost inevitably, affects his children adversely also. They sense their dad's guilt and can take unfair advantage of his vulnerability. Ex-wife Rosie talked about how this "shuttle diplomacy" affected her teenage son.

My wife-in-law simply refused to let my son have his friends over to her house. She told him he could have one friend, but *only* one. I guess she needs a lot of peace and quiet after a strenuous day of compulsive shopping. Anyway, my ex-husband went along with this rule—not wanting to make waves—but told our son he could use the house whenever they were away on weekends. Well, I thought that was a bad idea, even though it's not my house. Our son is sixteen, and who knows what could happen with no adults around. I trust him, yet I also had visions of scenes from *Risky Business*. I talked to my ex about it and expressed my concern. I think he's so worried about making up to our son for all the times he can't be there for him, that he forgets to be a real parent sometimes.

While many former wives had serious complaints about how their ex-husbands behaved toward them or their kids, there were those who spoke lovingly of their former mates. This residual bond of affection between former couples is often threatening to the current wife. Even though she has the license and the ring, she feels that the competition will never end. At the back of her mind lurks the fear that her husband still pines for his ex-wife, even more attractive now that she is forbidden fruit.

Divorced wives who still feel a connection to their mutual husbands don't necessarily want to return to their former status. But they do sometimes fill a special role as close friend and confidant. Some former wives said that their exes were "still family"—and that they felt a need to keep up with each other as they would with any close relative.

In former-wife Trudy's case, her ex-husband actually used to cry on her shoulder about his current wife. Their close ties as friends—and Trudy's acknowledgment that she and her ex couldn't live happily together as husband and wife—overrode their concerns about the current wife's jealousy.

> I often feel very defensive, very protective toward my ex-husband, particularly when my wife-in-law says something unkind about him. I have no desire to live with him again, but I don't want anyone hurting him either, because he's still a part of me. After all, I was married to him for twenty years. I don't think you can live with someone that long and share three children and not feel that he'll always be a part of you. He feels the same way and trusts me enough to discuss certain problems he's having with his new wife. I appreciate our closeness, yet I'm trying to convince him to see a marriage counselor with her, since talking to me won't really help their relationship.

This kind of closeness between former spouses can be a recipe for trouble. The current wife often worries that the lingering warm feelings the mutual husband has for his ex-wife will interfere with her new marriage, even when there's no real threat of the former couple reuniting. She may want to avoid conflict with her wife-in-law, but she doesn't, understandably, want her to be an intimate part of the new life. Most current wives strongly prefer that their husbands, to the extent possible, cut these ties to the past.

Molly found her husband's "best friend" relationship with his ex-wife annoying in itself, and even more so because he seemed to be pressuring her to follow suit.

> When I first started dating Gene, I thought it was odd that he kept wanting me to meet his first wife. He was anxious for me to like her and for us to become friends.

Their divorce had been a mutual decision—there was no sexual chemistry between them, but they were still bosom buddies. Even now, they talk on the phone at least once a week. Gene just helped her move into her new place, and he wants us to invite her for Christmas. I like her too, but I don't feel the need to incorporate her into my family. All I can say is, I'll be ecstatic when she finally meets the man of her dreams.

Not all current wives are as tolerant as Molly. She's secure enough in her relationship with Gene to allow him to continue his friendship with his ex-wife, and she doesn't seem to mind waiting it out until her wife-in-law finds a new mate. But I heard many current wives complain bitterly about how their wives-in-law behaved as if they were still married to their exes—calling them at all hours of the night to discuss personal problems, asking them to come over to fix a leaky roof or make other house repairs, making unannounced appearances at their ex-husband's office to talk over problems with the kids. "Remaining on a friendly basis is one thing," Lenora exclaimed, "but I think it's time for my husband and his ex-wife to realize they're not married anymore! *I'm* here for him now, and she'd be wise to start finding someone to take his place!"

Co-parenting

For many mutual husbands, the most wrenching experience associated with divorce and remarriage is the lost opportunity to be with their kids on a day-to-day basis. According to recent statistics, 90 percent of the children of divorce live with their mother. While shared custody is becoming a more popular option and weekend visits can be close, comfortable times together, most mutual husbands find themselves painfully divorced from the daily joys (and even irritations and problems) of parenting children from the earlier marriage.

Both current and ex-wives with whom I spoke revealed that

mutual husbands often expressed a longing to have their children live with them again. Similarly, sons and daughters alike yearn for the missing parent's approval and fantasize that life with them would be ideal and carefree. This is especially true of teenagers. Even where the family structure has remained stable, the teenager's life is complicated by the roller coaster of hormonal flux. Teenagers who have undergone the trauma of a family split are particularly vulnerable to such yearnings. Combine this with a father's desire for more co-parenting, and one solution seems obvious.

I heard many former wives extol the teens-living-with-dad plan, saying the timing couldn't be more perfect. "Let *them* teach the kids to drive, talk to them about sexual precautions, wait up till the wee hours to be sure they're home safe—I'll be glad to have some honest-to-goodness help during these hellish years," one former wife exclaimed.

When my own son was thirteen years old, he believed that his life would be perfect, all his problems alleviated, if only he could live with his father. In spite of his feelings, often expressed, I was reluctant to let him go. I'd miss him and was uncertain about the kind of home my ex-husband and wife-in-law would provide. But I didn't want to stand in his way. His strong conviction that living with his dad for six months was *the* answer convinced me that I just couldn't deny them the chance to get reacquainted on a day-to-day basis. Even though I felt I was being temporarily robbed of the most precious thing in my life, what was an extremely difficult time for me proved rewarding for everyone else. I know today that had I refused to cooperate, it would have been detrimental not only to my relationship with my son, but to the resolution of some of his separation issues with his father as well. I'm so glad now that I allowed it all to happen.

It's difficult for men to make up for years of absentee fathering with a temporary period of steady live-in attention; nevertheless, the experience can be hugely rewarding to parent and child. There are cases, however, when teenagers (and younger children as well) are allowed to become overly manipulative. Current-wife Christine described her situation with her stepson, Jeremy, as a "yo-yo kind of deal."

Jeremy is no different than a lot of other fifteen-year-olds. He's going through a phase where anything any adult recommends means zip. He's rebellious, withdrawn, and often depressed. His mom has had discussions ad nauseam with his dad about what to do. It seemed Jeremy kept harping on wanting to come and live with us for a while. Tim, of course, jumped on the idea. He misses his son a lot, even though we have him with us every other weekend. So we all agreed that Jeremy would move in with us and see his mom every other weekend—reversing the regular arrangement.

Things were great for about two weeks. But the first time Tim had to set limits—forbidding Jeremy to stay out later than midnight—Jeremy flipped out. He ranted and raved that Tim was a worse parent than Lisa, threw the divorce up in our faces, saying that's why he felt so screwed up, and promptly called his mom to tell her he wanted to come home. When she said no, he made a desperate plea, claimed he was "depressed" and intimated that he might commit suicide.

I don't take that kind of outpouring lightly, but I honestly think Jeremy was playing his dad against his mom. They both adore him and would do anything to please him, but even Tim could see that Jeremy was laying on the theatrics to get his way. So Jeremy stayed with us and moped around the house for about a week, and Tim tried continually to win him over. What was really sad was how much Tim needed Jeremy's approval and love. But the honeymoon was over. Tim had done a lot of fantasizing about how wonderful it would be to have his son back full time, but things haven't turned out the way he'd expected.

Those of us whose husbands are concerned, caring, involved fathers should be eternally grateful on behalf of our children and stepchildren. Children need their fathers in order to complete essential aspects of their emotional development—and fathers need their kids too.

Unspoken Messages

Despite the "new man's" reputed willingness to express his feelings more intimately to those he's close to, most wives-in-law agree that mutual husbands generally keep their emotions under wraps. The fact is that most men *and* women struggle with issues of personal and emotional honesty. So it's not surprising that mutual husbands keep their innermost feelings about the highly charged areas of divorce, remarriage, and parenting hidden, sometimes even from themselves. Voicing their deepest emotions might be overwhelming.

What happens, then, when mutual husbands repress anger, confusion, and pain? Some feelings get buried, other emotions spill over, and the message gets distorted. What should be articulated isn't, but the unspoken emotions still carry a sharp sting. Former-wife Marianne talked about what her former husband failed to communicate to her. In her case, as in many others, the failure is a mutual one.

Walt resents the fact that I demand the alimony that's due me. He thinks that since I have a good job and make decent money, I should let him off the hook. He finds it emasculating to send me my check when he could be impressing my wife-in-law—or the Barbie doll, as I call her—with a new car or a trip to Florida. I heard through my ex-brother-in-law that Walt thinks of me like the IRS—he has to fulfill his obligations, he knows he can't get out of them, but he doesn't have to like it. I guess since he can't do anything about the money he owes me, he figures he can shortchange me emotionally. What really burns me up is that in the five years since our divorce, he's never once complimented me on the good job I'm doing with our son. He won't ever give me the satisfaction of knowing I've done something right in his eyes. On the other hand, he goes overboard with our son—giving him extravagant gifts and taking him on little trips all the time—as a way of competing with me. I call all those goodies he gives Jimmy his "silent arsenal." The bottom line is, he fights me in these underhanded ways, but he's never been able to come right out and tell me what's going on inside. Whenever we see each other, everything is cool. We treat each other like polite strangers, but we're both seething inside.

Marianne's story isn't unique. Fortunately, in her case, things got better after they got worse. Her nine-year-old son was having problems in school, which led the family (including her ex-husband and wife-in-law) to seek therapy. Her ex-husband is learning to be more open about his resentment, Marianne is finding it easier to deal with a real person rather than a phantom adversary, and Jimmy is doing better now that some of the family "secrets" are out in the open.

The relationship between wives-in-law doesn't take place in a vacuum. How a mutual husband interacts—or doesn't interact—with both wives profoundly influences the connection between them. If he withdraws, the two women must go it alone, for better or worse. If he chooses instead to stir up trouble, wives-in-law often *react* to conflict rather than resolving it. When husbands attempt to mediate between their former and current wives, they may prevent the two women from dealing directly with important issues. And if the men are too friendly with their ex-wives, they risk alienating the women to whom they're currently married.

It may sound as if these men are in a no-win situation, but that's not entirely so. We've examined many of the most common problematic scenarios; but positive solutions to "sharing" a mutual husband do exist. The key seems to be honest, direct communication between as many parties as possible. And compromise. And patience. As with all aspects of the wife-in-law relationship, there are no ground rules for adjusting to the reality of a "mutual husband." There will always be awkward moments, unfulfilled expectations, hurt feelings. Nevertheless, wives and husbands alike must struggle to keep the lines of communication open, to deal frankly and respectfully with one another, to give in occasionally rather than giving up altogether.

Mutual husbands are an integral part of the family system. When they suffer or withdraw or harbor resentment, every member of the family is profoundly affected. On the other hand, when they decide to confront their concerns or problems head-on, when they begin to let go of blame and bitterness, the entire family benefits immeasurably.

Coping Strategies

I certainly don't set myself up as the best example of how to handle a wife-in-law relationship. If a good relationship means an interactive one, then I'd say I've done a pretty shabby job. Most of the time I've avoided dealing with my wife-in-law because, mercifully, we are separated by enormous geographical distances and blessed with a mutual husband who deals with me directly. My wife-in-law and I cope by not coping, and, as a result, we are stuck with the same stale problems and issues that we had ten years ago. No resolution—no growth.

Unlike me, 49 percent of the women in this research felt they handled the wife-in-law relationship capably; another 43 percent felt they coped about as well as could be expected; and only 7 percent admitted they dealt with things poorly. I've come to realize that although many women find themselves in situations similar to mine, their strategies for coping work far better.

Based on firsthand accounts, I've grouped these strategies into five coping styles:

1. Avoidance
2. Aggression
3. Civility
4. Compatibility
5. Blended Families

Of course, real life isn't as tidy as these five categories suggest; all of us mix and match them, depending on how the eight influential factors (see Chapter 3) shape our particular circumstances, but generally we prefer to interact using one at a time.

Difficulties can occur when wives-in-law don't share the same dominant style. For example, when the first wife plans to include her wife-in-law in a friendly backyard barbecue, and the current wife wants nothing but a Cold War, all hell can break loose. Or when a second wife wants to be deeply involved in the co-parenting of stepchildren, and the ex-wife diplomatically declines, a simmering resentment builds and sometimes boils over. In time, unspoken ground rules evolve to keep these volcanic emotions from erupting. Or, if a full-scale eruption does take place, many of us try to smooth it over and pretend it never happened. In either case, we generally don't dig deeply enough to get at the heart of the matter, and if we end up avoiding our wife-in-law, it's likely that she'll reciprocate. Our positions become entrenched and fossilized.

When we find ourselves in these frozen face-offs, our emotions block our ability to thaw the ways in which we relate to one another. Jealousy, competitiveness, resentment, and the need for revenge prevent our progress. Ultimately, we may surrender to our frustration and begin to believe in the Scarlett O'Hara version of the future: If we can get through today, tomorrow will be better and the unpleasantness may disappear altogether.

It's helpful to see how other women have coped with these impasses. If we understand what style of relating we now use with our wife-in-law, we can decide whether we want or need to change it.

AVOIDANCE:
When one wife-in-law banishes the other from her life, she becomes expert at denying feelings and blocking problems. "I don't wish her ill," says first-wife Ellen defensively, "she simply doesn't exist for me." Women like Ellen, who resents her husband's remarriage, long for physical distance between themselves and their wives-in-law. If they could ship them to another planet, they would.

A woman who has permanent amnesia about her wife-in-law's existence is, in some ways, more problematic to deal with than one whose hostility is up front. Passive-aggressive wives-in-law, though they may appear to be totally in control of the situation and invulnerable, are often terrified of their own anger and expend a great deal of energy burying their turbulent feelings. Beneath their icy facade, they may feel uncertain that their rage is justified and powerless to control it, so they deny its existence. Paradoxically, the more these feelings are bottled up, the more uncontrollable they become, like a powder keg ready to explode.

Few of us enjoy being around stockpiled ammunition. When these wives-in-law run into each other in public—at parties, work, family events, school activities—they rarely speak and sometimes refuse even to acknowledge the other's presence. "It takes enormous precision and energy to stay far enough away from my wife-in-law at PTA meetings," says Mandy. "Making sure we don't bump into one another or sit near each other is like being a commando in a mine field!"

Hannah, who has struggled with this kind of relationship with her wife-in-law for over eleven years, is at her wit's end and admits defeat.

I want her out of my life just as much as she has wanted me out of hers. She's won, or lost, depending on how you look at it. Her punishing disregard always left me feeling like a nonperson.

The straw that broke my back happened about

three weeks ago. I was at my favorite lingerie shop downtown treating myself to a new negligee, and the saleslady led me to a dressing room. She accidentally opened the wrong door and there was my wife-in-law trying on bras. I was catatonic. She looked right through me to the saleslady, handed her her rejects, and in a voice that would petrify Vampira, asked for a 34B in ivory, not white. She was stripped to the waist and, without missing a beat, turned back to the mirror and said something like, "Please shut the door, there's a draft." I shrunk back, speechless, and slinked away.

She has always had a way of making me feel like a second-class citizen—my guilt about marrying Sandy so soon after their divorce, plus her treating me as though I were a slut. She's always made me feel cheap. I even started to believe it was true. Now, I realize that the fullness in my life makes hers seem empty, and that makes her want to strike out and hurt me. Well, no more nice-guy stuff. It's my turn, I'm fed up, and I'm going to look out for myself. I've come to think of her as a nuclear waste dump . . . a place that's deadly, contaminating, and off-limits.

Hannah's wife-in-law has taken every opportunity to make her feel tainted and insignificant. As her wife-in-law's nearest moving target, Hannah may be entirely justified in sidestepping the firing range. In fact there are many women who insist that the only answer to this wife-in-law loggerheads is to steer clear.

Ultimately, there are battles in life that we will lose no matter what we do. Relationships don't always turn out as good, or even as tolerable, as we would like them to be. But if we know we've done our best to make them work, then sometimes, like Hannah, we must simply move on.

If, however, you are the wife-in-law who is withholding your feelings at all costs because you are scared to death to say the "wrong thing," terrified that if you express what you really feel you will leave irreparable devastation in your wake, you should remind yourself often that covert anger is far more destructive to ourselves and to others than "clean" anger that is out in the open.

If you have trouble in these areas you might consider reading books on assertiveness like *I'm O.K., You're O.K.* These works help us acknowledge and express the full range of our feelings in a more direct, less punishing way. As a first step, you might experiment with writing your feelings down in a private journal—for your eyes only—just to get an objective sense of your own emotions. Another option might be to join a support group where you can practice speaking your mind and letting yourself share your feelings rather than swallow them. Once you've started to rebuild your self-esteem, you will have less desire to waste time pretending your wife-in-law doesn't exist or playing the martyr.

AGGRESSION:

At first glance, wife-in-law relationships that are highly aggressive seem to be mirror opposites to those of avoidance. Yet these two coping styles are different sides of the same coin; both involve a need to internalize someone else's point of view in a desperate attempt to protect and preserve one's own. If one relies on first-strike tactics, it's possible to maintain the I'm-right-she's-wrong position without ever having to discover otherwise.

An aggressive wife-in-law is likely to be driven by unresolved anger and, deeper still, feelings of insecurity, fear, and frustration. A former wife who is aggressive might be saying to herself, *I may be the loser, but I'm going to go down fighting.* An aggressive current wife, who silently wonders how she stacks up against her husband's first wife, might be asking herself, *If I forced him to choose sides, would he choose mine?* In either case, the behavior of an aggressive wife-in-law screams out, *I am more powerful; I am in control; I am the better wife!*

Women who use this style employ all kinds of assaultive behavior, or the threat of it, at outrageous times and places. I am not referring to straightforward, healthy anger; these are the hysterical screamers, the drama queens who create public scenes and private anguish with the heavy club of humiliation, abuse, and fear. In some ways this style is a form of terrorism; those who suffer its recriminations live with the threat of the next incident which will trigger another mortar barrage. Former-wife Heddy knows this scenario only too well.

> One minute it's, "Hi, how are you doing," and the next minute when I come to pick up my kid, I can hear my wife-in-law say, "Well, here comes the witch!"
>
> Little Ari is usually crying, not knowing what to expect. He ends up wetting his pants and refuses to talk for the next three hours because he is so anxious about what might happen the next time I take him back to his dad's. My wife-in-law doesn't care what kind of psychological damage she inflicts on him, just as long as she can vent her bitterness on me.
>
> When she attacks, it takes everything I have to continue to behave like a lady. I know she's dying for me to get down to her level, but there is so much other bad stuff going on I don't want to play into her antics. She'll just have to be the "Erica" on her own petty soap opera. It's too rough on my son and just isn't worth it.

This painful situation has several short-term remedies. Heddy might redefine the contact with her wife-in-law by asking a friend to come along when she picks up Ari. The presence of a third party might encourage her wife-in-law to be on better behavior. Failing this, Heddy will have the support of her friend, to buffer her wife-in-law's hostility.

Heddy might also try explaining Ari's reactions to her ex-husband. He might be able to intervene or at least share responsibility for transporting his son back and forth.

If Heddy is willing to risk an unpleasant confrontation, she might consider speaking directly to her wife-in-law, or writing her a letter, describing her distress. She might start with something like, "I know you are angry with me. I'd like to know what the problem is so that we can get to the bottom of it. It is just too difficult on Ari and me, on all of us, to keep on this way. We should meet and talk this out between ourselves (or with our clergyperson/counselor/trusted friend) and try to work things out."

Gutsy, yes! Disarming, absolutely! But if the communication is clear, open, firm, and consistent, there is the possibility that it will help clear the air. But beware, some wives-in-law prefer all-out war because it is clear-cut, the good guys against the bad. An aggressive wife-in-law prefers living in the war zone; battle lines are plainly drawn and there is no murky business of polite conversation or civil behavior to the "enemy." This position forces everyone involved to choose sides; there is no neutral territory, no innocent bystanders.

If you do choose to fight back, however, be prepared for a no-win situation. As offense meets offense, as adversaries dig in and tempers flare, no one thinks clearly, and little is accomplished. Furthermore, a wife-in-law who is a pro at the aggression strategy is a formidable opponent. When she "loses it" or "acts out" she often blames her misconduct on forces beyond her control, like alcohol, the abominable character of her wife-in-law, or the personality traits of their mutual husband. For such women, it's much easier to make someone else the villain than to sort out the real issues involved. Easier perhaps, but absolutely exhausting and unproductive for everyone. Imagine being on the receiving end of former-wife Muriel's torment.

Whoever said revenge isn't sweet never had a wife-in-law! I push her buttons whenever I get even the hint of a chance. The other night I called and implied that my ex was lying about something that I knew she was insecure about. I just planted a little seed, something to egg her on and get her going. We got into a screaming match on the phone and then I just hung up. It was a small moment of glory for all the hurt that I've been through!

There are times when I fantasize about how I'm going to get her goat next time. I've thought of down-and-dirty things like putting Nair in her shampoo or letting the air out of her tires at the supermarket. Not that I would necessarily do either, mind you! Those fantasies help me vent and are an endless source of satisfaction.

These violent feelings that thrive on unresolved rage make everyone feel they are looking right over the edge; they damage and estrange the ones they love.

Under conditions of extreme hostility, normalizing relations and bridging disagreements takes enormous effort and commitment. Muriel's wife-in-law can resort to a number of options. First, she can ignore Muriel outright and hope that these vicious feelings will burn themselves out. Admittedly this takes internal fortitude and patience! Second, the current wife can enlist the support of her husband by asking him to help her find ways to reach her assaultive wife-in-law in order to defuse the situation.

Finally, if it looks as if it is possible to initiate a dialogue, do some homework ahead of time and prepare a "problem sheet" summarizing what you'd like to say about how you see the situation, how you'd like it to be different, and what the options are from your point of view.

Remember to keep your scripted expectations realistic—these problems weren't created overnight and they won't get resolved that quickly either. And even if things don't work out perfectly, at the very least, you've tried.

CIVILITY:

Civility, in the words of one wife-in-law, is "the courteous side of tolerance—and tolerance where your wife-in-law is concerned is nothing more or less than the ability to roll with the punches—even if she never ceases to irritate you in some way!" This wife-in-law style requires humor, forbearance, and respect for your wife-in-law's boundaries and her right to her own opinions. Current or ex-wives who cope with their counterparts civilly don't hide the fact that this strategy is not without its share of frustration, discomfort, or awkwardness. But once they discover that one polite word leads to another, they're hooked! Arlette, a convert to civility, says, "Practice doesn't make the relationship perfect, but it does make it less painful."

The civil course depends on cooperative communication, conciliatory moves and concessions, and most of all, a mature sense of responsibility on the part of both wives-in-law. On the most practical level, becoming more civil to one another means having some self-knowledge—understanding your own buttons and being able to exercise self-control when your wife-in-law pushes them. Arlette, a current wife, uses the time-honored technique of "biting my tongue if I'm about to say something that I know will blow things sky-high!"

Developing this kind of self-control in order to build a relationship with a wife-in-law who is approaching the interaction from another perspective, with different motivations, is a challenge. But the operative word here is "developing"—keeping in mind that the relationship is in flux and continually being changed and refined. For everyone involved there must be a willingness to listen and to accept. Arlette explains further.

I still don't agree with my wife-in-law even half the time, but she is a fact of my life and I can't wish her away. My husband and I share custody of their twelve-year-old daughter, Jessie, so we are all in constant contact. She and I are pretty close and there are lots of times that I forget I'm only her stepmom.

About a year and a half ago, Jessie and I were driving in the car and I let slip a supercritical remark about her mother, something about her not having a very good head about the way she managed her money.

Jessie's eyes welled up with tears and she said, "Mom never says any bad stuff about you even though you treat her like she doesn't exist—she isn't made of steel, you know!"

I felt so ashamed of myself and realized that I had never really given Inga, my wife-in-law, the time of day, even though she had attempted some initial openings by asking me if Jessie was behaving herself or giving me any trouble. I can't lie and say I ever even tried to be friendly. My standard response to her was more like a door slamming. But I thought I was being a lot more subtle about it, and I never realized that Jessie noticed my cold shoulders and chilly replies. But once I saw her tears, I didn't want to risk losing any more of her respect than I already had.

So over the last nine months I have tried to shift my attention away from Inga's grating habits—like when she returns Jessie's lunch box and it's dirty. It's the bigger stuff that counts . . . it's Jessie who counts.

I still run hot and cold on my wife-in-law, but I am making more of a genuine effort to be polite and to engage her in conversation about Jessie's well-being. When I drop Jessie off I take a few moments to check in with Inga instead of getting out of earshot as soon as I can. The times that she does start to get to me, I silently count to ten and by the time I've finished I can say good-bye politely.

I know Inga has no desire to be buddy-buddy with me, nor do I with her, just civil. And it's amazing how some basic manners between adult women can make the difference as to whether a child smiles or not.

Many wives-in-law redouble their efforts to smooth things over if children are involved. Other women tell of icebreaking events that forced communication between them. Hope and Daphne surprised themselves after spending twenty-six grueling hours in the labor room together with Daphne's daughter, who was delivering her first child.

Neither Hope nor I had slept much, we were both worried sick about Annie's sluggish contractions, and when that baby came out, we were shocked to find ourselves hugging and crying out of joy and relief. We got through that one without one spark between us, and decided that it wouldn't be good for baby Brad if we continued to act like gunslinging grandmas.

After the birth, we made an unspoken peace pact. Now whenever we see each other we're so busy goo-gooing the baby that those good feelings become the focus rather than the bad ones.

Civility, particularly if there is a history of estrangement between wives-in-law, takes a conscious effort and a genuine desire to achieve even comfortable relations. But, like every change, it doesn't come easy or fast. Current-wife Janice ironically adds, "Now that I've finally gotten to the point where I can have polite conversation with my wife-in-law, I look back and think that this was my Mt. Everest. Even my marriage to my ex was easier! In fact, if I'd been this courteous to him, we probably would have stayed married!"

COMPATIBILITY:

Wives-in-law who use this coping style demonstrate the ability to take a sincerely sympathetic view toward each other's problems and families. At the same time, these women are also firmly grounded in their own separate lives and marriages. Wives-in-law who are compatible take care to acknowledge and honor their common bonds but are mindful not to meddle or invest too much emotional energy in their wife-in-law's family when it might be inappropriate or unwelcome. For example, unsolicited opinions or comments about the mutual husband's character faults or sexual shortcomings are usually verboten. "We laughed

and cried our way through the awkward moments at the beginning," says Sue Ellen. "I'd make a faux pas and then she'd make
a bigger one, but that's how we learned not to step on each
other's toes. Once we actually kept a tally of all the times we
had each stuck a foot in our mouth. We figured it was a draw.
At that point we stopped counting forever!"

In a broader sense, by knowing their own limits and the
limitations of the relationship, these wives-in-law are freer to
offer help to one another. It is a process of trial and error, but
those who have achieved compatibility are proud of their bond.

Maria, a current wife, describes the evolution of her unlikely relationship with her wife-in-law, Camille. Through a
quirk of fate they came to trust each other for the first time and
were able to establish an emotional foundation of mutual support
during an unforeseen crisis.

> Camille and I were on shaky ground at first, neither of
> us knew how to act with the other. Even my mother-
> in-law, who loves us both, used to make cutting
> remarks about Camille in order to make me feel wel-
> come in the family. It's pretty funny, now that I look
> back, because neither of us really feels threatened by
> the other. I think of Camille as just another member
> of the family.
>
> Our first chance to get to know one another came
> as a fluke. My stepson was getting married in a small
> town in Vermont. One hundred guests were scheduled
> to arrive for the wedding but the hotel had gotten the
> date wrong. The entire place was overbooked, so
> Camille, our stepdaughter, and I ended up sharing one
> room while the men bunked together in another part
> of the hotel. Our stepdaughter went partying that
> evening, so Camille and I were alone for the first time.
> We knew it was going to be an all-nighter, so we
> ordered room service. When the tray was delivered the

waiter asked that Mrs. X sign the check. We looked at each other and burst out laughing. That broke the ice.

Then we got to work. She and I hunkered down like a SWAT team—booking another hotel for the reception, scaling down the menu, tracking down a band to play, ordering the flowers. Meanwhile, between cups of coffee and bathroom runs, we were swapping stories about our lives. By the wee hours of the morning, we had reorganized the wedding from the ground up and knew a hell of a lot about each other. We took that opportunity to build a tentative friendship instead of feeding our animosity, and I found that I liked her in spite of all my preconceived ideas. Unfortunately, other more serious problems have come up, like our mutual husband's alcoholism. His near-fatal car accident shook both of us up, and so she started looking into Al-Anon and suggested we both go.

The hardest part was coming to terms with how we were both feeding his addiction. Camille had spent years in her former marriage covering his tracks and I was into a really heavy case of denial. I just couldn't face the fact that I had married an alcoholic until he started getting abusive with me. Then I knew it was time to take off the blinders. Camille and I went to our first meeting together and cried all the way home. It's given us a special bond—a deeper connection that wouldn't have happened otherwise. Ironically, it's our mutual husband's disease that brought us closer together.

She gives me full credit for his recovery, but the real credit goes to my husband. He was ready, and we were ready to face it with him.

Granted we have our separate lives and boundaries, and that makes our relationship clearer . . . no double messages. But when it comes to shared concerns, I listen to hers and she listens to mine. Even though we may disagree, we work together, not against each other.

When some of the other wives-in-law at our group meetings heard these stories of compatibility, there was disbelief, a touch of jealousy, and more than a hint of resentment. "They're either very healthy or very crazy," scoffed one wife-in-law, shaking her head. This reaction was shared by others who felt as if friendly wives-in-law had betrayed the fold!

And, in some significant ways, they had. Compatible wives-in-law do relate to one another differently. First of all, they strive, not always successfully but determinedly, to work toward the best possible relationship by:

- trying to understand differences
- talking through matters of mutual concern
- being reliable and following through on commitments and promises
- accepting and learning from one another

Even more importantly, compatible wives-in-law feel that they are role models for their children. Lois explains.

You have to try to make peace between you. If you try and it fails, that's one thing. But if you don't make that first effort, then you never find out if things could be different. And that's the whole nut right there— knowing you can make things different. That goes for friendships, marriages, divorces—even wives-in-law.

I want my kids to have successful marriages. But even if they don't, at least they'll have a positive example of adults trying hard to work things out, and my wife-in-law and I will deserve some of the credit for that.

BLENDED FAMILIES:
Blended families offer us the possibility of new definitions of "relatedness. " They resemble the more traditional extended family of the past but go further by bending the conventional notions of who qualifies as kin and who doesn't. Extending the kin network to include these more distant "relatives" adds a new wrinkle to the face of modern-day families. For example, Nora thinks of her wife-in-law's stepbrother's stepchildren as a welcomed part of the clan.

In the course of this research, I came upon a handful of blended families that were perfectly intermingled and it was clearly the relationship between the wives-in-law that had brought the families together. The wives-in-law of blended families were unwilling to give up the benefits of family life and were absolutely committed to preserving that special sense of closeness that might otherwise be destroyed or undermined by divorce.

Although there seems to be a fine line between compatibility and blended wife-in-law relationships, each of these wives-in-law had thought through the pros and cons. Sometimes such a merging was regarded as a mixed blessing. At first, Charlotte, an ex-wife, had wondered if getting this close to her wife-in-law meant that she was still clinging to her former marriage. But two things happened to quiet her fears. Charlotte became more secure in her own remarriage, and she began to know and respect Nora independent of her ex-husband.

As unorthodox or unlikely as it might seem, the first choice of these wives-in-law was to be friends, confidants, and kin. They liked each other and each other's children; they sometimes planned family holidays and vacations together and spoke frequently during the week just to catch up.

Charlotte, the first wife, and Nora, the current one, offered me a fascinating insight into their version of a blended family. Charlotte began the story.

Some people have called us weird and I can see why, since most divorced families hate one another. But I consider us trailblazers, and we are not going to let other people's ideas about divorce stand in our way.

I'm not sure how it all came about, but I do remember about five years ago starting to have lunch regularly with my ex-husband so that we could continue parenting our five children in a responsible way. Nora was welcome to come from the beginning, but she knew that it was going to be more like a stockholders' meeting than a social chat and felt fine about Keith and me getting together for what were really business meetings. These lunches expanded into family gatherings which included the whole crew, and they were surprisingly joyful. Eventually my husband, Stan, and Nora and Keith decided we should get together without the children, for no particular occasion. We even went camping together, just the four of us. It has been a yearly tradition ever since.

Acquaintances who've heard about us think there is something kinky going on. To tell you the truth, we really don't much care—how can we help what other people think? But there are times when the innuendos and curiosity are overwhelming. On occasion, church meetings make Stan uncomfortable. It's not that he is embarrassed; he just doesn't want to be explaining the situation constantly. Our most important barometers are our children. I love Nora's children—I think of them as mine—and my kids love her. I've had long talks with my kids, and they somehow understand that Keith makes a better friend for me than a husband. We also get a lot of support from in-laws. Keith's parents adore Stan, and I've become much closer to them since my parents died.

Nora contributed her side of the story.

> Charlotte and I went shopping last week for dresses for her daughter's wedding. We are planning to light the bride's unity candle together at the ceremony. My wife-in-law and I are friends because we are lucky enough to have genuine interest in one another; we just like doing things together.
>
> Our relationship really solidified once Charlotte got remarried; then everything relaxed and opened up. That's not to say we don't have our boundaries. We don't compare notes about Keith or our sex lives. We don't revisit the past much and haven't gotten into many fault-finding arguments. Charlotte and I know each other so well that we don't have to poke around in each other's lives.
>
> We have mutual respect, and part of that grows out of how Charlotte and Keith handled their divorce. It was not a throat-slashing party; they were honorable toward one another. It helped everyone forgive the pain and loss.
>
> People are always trying to make a wedge between us. For example, some have asked me if I'm jealous that Charlotte's financial situation has improved since her marriage to Stan. I've told them that she's so terrific that she deserves to get what she wants. It makes things even better between us when she is happy.

By the time both women finished their stories, my head was spinning. When I stood back and reflected on what they had told me, I realized they had given me the cornerstones of a blended family. Charlotte and Nora had:

- mutual respect
- a personal commitment to the wife-in-law relationship and to making it better

- open communication
- a supportive network of family and friends who accepted and encouraged them

I listened carefully to Charlotte and Nora, thinking that perhaps this kind of amicable arrangement might seem less freakish in the future. With the wife-in-law phenomenon affecting at least a third of our population, we are moving in a questionable direction—in the worst case toward a society of divided, warring families. Blended families are the other extreme. Most of us, with more modest goals, fall somewhere in between, and we should feel satisfied with each step we make toward a more comfortable relationship with our wife-in-law.

Blended families aren't for everyone. But if we are seeking constructive role models for future wives-in-law, this one is certainly worth serious consideration.

Turning Points

Assessing the Relationship

Ultimately, it's the unrelenting, gnawing combination of resentment and helplessness that we seek to remedy. We ask ourselves continually, "Why me?" We look to our children and ask, "Why them?" The seeming absence of answers with staying power reinforces our frustrations and anger.

I asked the women in this survey, "Looking back, would you do things differently in your relationship with your wife-in-law?" Eighty-eight percent of former wives and 77 percent of current wives answered with a resounding, "Yes!" They had floundered in their attempts to cope, opened doors only to shut them again, and built up walls only to tear them down. They'd stumbled, fallen, gotten up and dusted themselves off, and through trial and error pioneered solutions again and again.

If they could relive their wife-in-law relationship from the beginning, they'd change it in a thousand different ways: "I'd level with her" versus "I wouldn't give her the time of day." "I'd be more supportive" rather than "I'd lobotomize her!" About half the former wives wished they had been more open and cooperative, less eager to heap the blame for their unhappiness on their wife-in-law. While some women admitted that they never tried hard enough in the first place, a sizable number said they became unwilling adversaries because their wives-in-law had never given *them* a chance. But the other 50 percent of first wives, and an even larger proportion of current wives, stated just the opposite. If they could do it over, they would insist on completely separate lives from the beginning, wouldn't be so tolerant of or vulnerable to their wives-in-law, and would ignore the relationship completely.

On the other hand, 18 percent of the women were basically satisfied with the way in which they had managed their wife-in-law relationships. Many didn't believe that the relationship would have been different, regardless of how they behaved, and so felt justified for not having tried to make things better.

The sad truth is that, for the majority of women who had made persistent efforts of goodwill, the wife-in-law relationship has never delivered, regardless of their investment. And each woman has had to make that final reckoning as to whether her emotional concessions have been worth the gains. Too often the payoff has been too little, too late.

I can't begin to count the number of personal interviews in which wives-in-law prefaced their comments with, "My circumstance is unique" or, "I know I'm not typical." While these individual stories are one-of-a-kind, each offers a vantage point to look inside struggles that may resemble our own. When we can see how another woman has come to terms with hurtful situations, struggled to find her own level of comfort, and arrived at a personal resolution, we can again look into ourselves with a fresh perspective.

When I use the term "personal resolution," I mean focusing first on doing what is necessary to find peace within ourselves before we even attempt more satisfying relations with our wife-in-law. In this research, 50 percent of former wives and 30 percent of current wives say that the overall nature of their wife-in-law relationship is comfortable. But that leaves a majority of women for whom the relationship is still awkward or painful.

The two most common obstacles to a better relationship were the inability to forgive and the inability to conquer the debilitating emotions of jealousy, resentment, and bitterness.

The inability to forgive is a tough one for each and every one of us, and many women speak of it as if it were utterly impossible. How often we've heard or said that we can forgive but not forget, yet based on this research neither is easy. Not only are wives-in-law downright hard on each other, they are even harder on themselves. It is not until we can find the ability to be at peace with ourselves that we can forgive others. It can't be emphasized too much: This self-acceptance is an essential cornerstone of personal resolution.

Seeking Professional Help

In order to make progress, we must look at the full range of options, tested and untried, familiar and outside our experience. For ex-wives self-change might well take the form of finally ending the relationship or obsession with the ex-husband. For current wives self-change might mean taking an inventory of unrealistic marriage expectations or identifying misplaced anger. In the course of listening to wives-in-law tell their stories, I soon discovered that many discussions of self-change led to explorations of the role of professional counseling.

I found many strong advocates for seeking professional help among the women in this survey. Wives-in-law, struggling with the many problems of divorce and remarriage, had gone alone or with family members, with varying degrees of commitment and effectiveness, to ministers, marriage counselors, self-help groups, psychologists, and psychiatrists. I talked to women who went as a last resort, to find personal assurance and reassurance that they had done everything they could under difficult circumstances, and to women who cried out for help in the middle of the night in desperation. I talked to women who had never sought coun-

seling before and wished they had, and to a tiny minority who
had and wished they hadn't—all trying to cope: to handle things
better, to hang in longer, to get through another day. Wilma, a
first-timer in therapy, wisely testifies.

> It hurts to go to counseling because it's traumatic to
> stir up all the buried scars that are deep and ugly. But
> once you tell it, once you get it out, it starts to go,
> and you can see that you will be able to start over. But
> there are no magic wands. All of it is still there, but I
> can deal with it and say, "Hey, that's the way it *was*,"
> and go on from there. I don't have to go on blaming
> or pointing the finger because no one wanted to listen
> or pay attention to my side of the story. The therapist
> is like a good parent who has no personal agenda other
> than listening and helping you grow up and lead a
> better, happier life. I can't recommend it enough.

Several women shared their problem of getting husbands or
ex-husbands to participate in counseling, although in a few cases
the men had initiated the idea. But more often, if the husbands
went at all, they went under protest. No one can drag anyone to
counseling against his will and expect it to work. Janice talked
about how persuading her husband to enter therapy actually
created an opportunity to free herself from a lifelong burden.

> The way I was raised, divorce is worse than any four-
> letter word. You see, I'm Catholic, and I guess I've
> never believed in divorce, so when my marriage was in
> real trouble I knocked myself out to save it. After
> months of nagging, I finally got my husband to go with
> me to see a counselor, but the minute we walked into
> the office he would seal off like King Tut's tomb.
> Afterward, he'd say, "You wanted me to go to that
> shrink, and I went."
>   It was painfully clear that it was really hard for

him to open up with his gut feelings, inside or outside the counselor's office. There was no way I was going to give up, but the catch is that honesty has to be a two-way street to work. So the more I asked him to be honest, the more I failed. The more I failed, the more I felt I was to blame. I was guilt-ridden the first two years after my divorce and begged him to come back even after I knew he was about to remarry. I wanted a chance to make up for all the things I had done wrong. I went back to the counselor as a last resort, thinking she would help me figure out a way to get my husband back. But she didn't mince words or mess around. She told me I was slowly killing myself by taking complete responsibility for everyone and everything—that I wasn't Superwoman and that even Superwoman had to learn to say good-bye.

Therapy gave me a place to practice, yes practice, saying good-bye to my husband and my marriage. My therapist used a lot of visualization in which I imagined my ex sitting in front of me, carrying on the conversation I always wanted to have. In that imaginary meeting I was able to tell him what I resented, what I regretted, and what I remembered fondly about our marriage.

And then, one day, in session with my therapist, I was finally ready to say good-bye, even though he never actually heard me. I could barely speak through my tears, but I heard myself uttering those parting words—as if I would never see him again. All of those pretend farewells have helped me begin to mourn for my loss so I can now carry on with my life and say good-bye for good.

Saying good-bye, as painful as it was, was Janice's way of saying to herself, *I did my best. I learned from this experience and I am better for it!* Once Janice let go of her husband, she was able to let go of her idea that her husband's new wife was the "winner" and that she was the "loser." When Janice stopped acting as though she were in a one-down position, she and her wife-in-law had their first decent conversation. "It was the first time I didn't desperately need anything she had, and she knew it," Janice said. "We were peers, the power struggle was over, and we could concentrate on working to get the family back on track."

When families seek counseling together, the therapist can use the varying perspectives of the participating members to piece together the mosaic of family interaction. When the family and its problems are seen as a system, it is possible to untangle the web of unhealthy patterns and dysfunctional relationships. The goal is to clarify for the family the ways in which it works against itself so that, both as a unit and individually, they can relearn healthier ways to relate to one another. Trudy's ex-husband and his current wife join her intermittently for sessions with her children. Their collective commitment gives them an excellent opportunity in which to gain insights into the damaging ways they relate to one another.

> It's amazing how much surfaces between my ex-husband and me even now . . . though we have been divorced for so long. He has hung on in therapy for the sake of the kids but still has a hard time sitting there with all of us and the counselor talking about painful realities. He would like everyone to believe that everything is wonderful. I used to think that he was an eternal optimist, but now I know he is into some heavy denial. Even Trish, his current wife, is beginning to see a side she never knew before. She'll sit in session and talk about how the kids are driving her crazy, and he'll tell her that there is nothing to worry about. Then he'll add that she and I are like two peas in a pod and say that I was always looking for the worst in everything too.

When that first came out of his mouth both our eyes popped out of our heads . . . Trish discovered something about her marriage, and I learned something about my divorce. It turns out that both of us felt very much alone whenever there were problems. With him so busy wishing things away, we had each started doubting our own sanity. Were we imagining problems or not?

Trish and I were equally relieved to find that we were in the same boat and bailing as fast as we could! But it makes us both wonder about him and whether it's possible to have a sane divorce or a sane marriage with this guy.

While Trudy was developing a deeper perspective on her former marriage, Trish was confronted with some frightening possibilities. Was she simply rewashing the dirty laundry of her husband's failed marriage? Family therapy revealed some pre-existing issues that threatened Trish's new marriage. But with the determination to get to the bottom of things, Trish came away with some fundamental insights that have literally transformed the way she and her husband deal with the challenges before them. Trish courageously took her head out of the sand and not only saved her marriage but got a real partner in the deal.

My new husband and I were almost as happy as clams when we went into family therapy with his ex-wife Trudy and the kids. Sure we had some hot spots between us, but I was very busy being the giddy newlywed and was just as guilty as my husband when it came to sweeping things under the rug. We went into therapy at my wife-in-law's urging, and when Trudy started raising some nasty resentments, I got pretty nervous and wanted to quit going. The last thing I wanted was to fall off my little cloud, but my husband insisted that we continue because it would help the children.

One thing led to another and I finally blurted out that my husband was like a wall when it came to dealing with everyday problems—like when one of the kids got out of hand. Trudy jumped on the same bandwagon with a vengeance! So there we were ganging up on this poor guy! Fortunately, the therapist intervened and suggested that Trudy and I consider how we both expected this one man to solve everything.

No wonder my husband couldn't face our complaints. He was terrified that he might fail. But if he pretended it wasn't a problem to begin with, he was safe.

This helped destroy his first marriage, and there it was in mine. So I had a choice. I could either learn how to offer him help with problems, big or little, without demanding or expecting instant solutions, or I could create the replica of the unhappy marriage he had left!

Although it was a hard truth to face so early in our marriage, I think my husband and I got a head start on some major problems that were bound to explode sooner or later. We are more committed than ever to finding all the energy and staying power it takes to work things through in therapy and in our marriage.

In Trudy and Trish's case, therapy provided both women with a better understanding of themselves and what had led, or was leading, to problems in their respective marriages. Trudy was able to view her former marriage with less self-blame and more closure than ever before. And Trish, although faced with the frightening possibility that what she learned in therapy might

lead to a second divorce, found unexpected strength to fortify
her marriage and build a deeper intimacy with her new husband.

Yet wives-in-law were not all pro-therapy. Some women
with whom I spoke wished they had never gone into therapy,
had doubts about its effectiveness and were disenchanted for a
number of reasons. Some felt that the therapeutic process was
too slow and too expensive; others had difficulty finding compe-
tent professionals.

The most common criticism I heard was that the counseling
was not sufficiently prescriptive. "I seemed to be encouraged to
keep talking until I found the answers," said one woman, "but
the problem was that the answers weren't inside of me. I needed
guidance and training." This woman, and others, found emotional support in peer groups, particularly Al-Anon and a parental support group she eventually located that was affiliated with
her church. She concluded that, for her, a spiritual component
was a necessary catalyst in the change process and was central to
her healing. "I saw a lot of women becoming very hardened in
support groups without a spiritual temper. Sometimes you feel
victimized for so long that you can't help but merge your own
anger with the group's—you can come out being militant and
even more angry than before. If you surrender your rage to a
higher power, no matter what or who that is, it frees you to do
the work that's needed: making amends and finding a way to
relate more lovingly."

If you're lucky enough, or patient and persistent enough, to
find the right counselor or group, and if you are open to the
process and its potential for help, then professional counseling
can, indeed, work wonders. Countless people attest to this.
However, if you've had unfruitful experiences and are ready to
abandon the idea of counseling or group sessions, or if you simply
feel it's not right for you, you might want to try other forms of
"therapy": Carla's weekly tennis game, Edna's once-a-year ad-
venture trek, or Beatrice's relaxing reading. Whatever works for
you, do it!

Turning Points

In the course of our lives, we can identify moments, sometimes a string of occurrences, that transform the way we've thought about or experienced something; so, too, in the lives and relationships of wives-in-law. When wives-in-law seize the initiative to clarify their own feelings and actions toward their counterparts, they cross the threshold toward emotional health. I define these thresholds as turning points, and they come in every imaginable form, at unexpected junctures, with unanticipated results.

To begin with, not all wife-in-law turning points necessarily have happy endings, some just have healthier ones. Hannah and Heddy, whom we met in Chapter 8, transformed negative situations into positive ones by taking self-preserving steps after successive destructive encounters with their wives-in-law obliterated any hope of redeeming the relationship. Remember, Hannah reclaimed her self-worth after realizing she was slowly destroying herself by pursuing a relationship with a wife-in-law who clearly didn't want one. And similarly, Heddy successfully maintained her self-respect by systematically refusing to play according to her wife-in-law's aggressive rules; "she was like a mud wrestler, and I just wouldn't get into the ring!"

More conciliatory truces between wives-in-law were often initiated through ordinary encounters: women finally managing to be in the same room with each other without breaking into a cold sweat, or being able to stand next to one another at a social event and actually to speak a civil word or two. These seemingly "insignificant" moments represented landmarks in wife-in-law relations.

Other wives-in-law experienced dramatic events that triggered cathartic release of pent-up anger and ill will. This was true for Sybil, who had endured seventeen years of enmity for both her adulterous ex-husband and her ex-mother-in-law, Bertha, who had been his alibi. On the day of Bertha's funeral,

Sybil broke through her bitterness and finally laid her own suffering to rest.

I went to the graveside kicking and screaming. If it hadn't been for my kids, I would have boycotted the funeral. But they were wiser than I, and insisted I go. When I divorced my husband for cheating on me, my ex-mother-in-law protected her "Darling Warren" from any kind of recriminations—she made it all my fault. She always said that he wouldn't have strayed if I had been a better wife. Warren believed her and used that excuse to defend himself for years.

Even though in my heart of hearts I knew differently, I left the marriage in a state of guilt, under the tyranny of their accusations. Warren never admitted his infidelities and never showed any remorse, any sense of loss, and his mother backed him all the way!

When Warren remarried, Bertha welcomed my wife-in-law as though she were the daughter she never had. She conducted a smear campaign against me, so from Day One my wife-in-law treated me like an outcast. Both Warren and Bertha cast dark shadows over my entire existence, like two Darth Vaders, self-righteous and unforgiving. I always considered my wife-in-law a part of the enemy camp. Sometimes I thought she was no better than Bertha's clone.

At Bertha's funeral my ex-husband was blind with grief. It was the first time I'd ever seen him cry. I imagine he was now afraid that he'd have to come out from behind Bertha's armor and face his own frailties. No more mama to make all the bad goblins go away!

When I passed by the open coffin and caught sight of her shrunken body, "Booming Bertha," as I used to call her, lost her grip on me. Something lifted—and it wasn't her spirit going to heaven! I experienced myself healthy, strong, and full of life, powerful in my own right, ready finally to leave my bitterness at the foot of her grave. And when I glanced over at the family room and caught sight of my wife-in-law weeping, I realized that, even through her mourning veil, she no longer resembled Bertha in the slightest.

Death, the great equalizer, sharpens our awareness of our own lives and those whom we love—and hate. In much the same way, the breakup of a second marriage can encourage both current and former wives to reexamine old beliefs and prejudices and to seek new truths about themselves and their counterparts. For example, Sybil begrudgingly acknowledged that, in the end, her wife-in-law had suffered a dismal fate that was not unlike her own. Their mutual ex-husband had been cheating on his second wife during her pregnancy and a few weeks after the baby's birth announced that he wanted a divorce. When his second wife learned that he planned to marry yet a third time, she understood all too well how devastating it was to have a husband leave you for another woman. Not only was the shoe on the other foot, but it fit! She telephoned Sybil full of remorse for having been the "other woman" the first time around. Sybil confided, "While I wasn't ready to say all was forgiven, I was certainly in a more conciliatory frame of mind toward her."

When former wives clucked about the termination of their husbands' subsequent marriages—or even rumors that the remarriage wasn't all coos and kisses—they admitted to feeling, if not outright pleasure, smug satisfaction. "I knew then that it wasn't all *me!*"

Remarriage statistics corroborate the gut reactions of these former wives. Second marriages are ending sooner, and tend to dissolve after a shorter period of time than do first marriages. The 1985 Current Population Survey data show that in that year, for example, the median interval between first marriage and first divorce was 7.5 years for women between the ages of 15 and 74, while the median interval between remarriage and redivorce was 4.9 years.[1]

An ex-husband's redivorce can serve as a reality check for the former wife who took on herself the full brunt of the disintegration of marriage or family or came to question her legitimate motives for seeking a divorce. The validation produced by the realization that "it wasn't just me" enabled these women, even after a long period of time, to stop blaming themselves. They no longer envied, distorted, or glamorized their wife-in-law's situation as better than their own, and this state of mind and emotion can be truly liberating.

Sometimes, though this occurs infrequently, the consequence of an ex-husband's redivorce is a bonding between ex-wives. Women who have a mutual ex-husband sometimes find comfort and support in shared experience. For example, two women in this survey formed a friendship with each other and the ex-wife of their former husband's brother—the "ex-related," they call themselves—and get together periodically simply to socialize.

More than one woman was motivated to transform her life based on a reawakened spirituality. Informal prayer, religious reaffiliation, or a communion with nature, to mention just a few, provided many women with the strength and will to reshape their personal relationships and try to resolve any ongoing conflicts with their wives-in-law. Delores is one example.

I had gone to church as a child but never really developed a formal belief. I could tell you all the things you were supposed to know about the Bible, but spiritual things didn't mean much to me until I found God for myself.

It was several years after my divorce, and, for no apparent reason, I was having a very emotional time. I cried a lot and couldn't understand why. My kids were healthy and doing particularly well at the time. I was dating a nice guy and my life seemed to be going along pretty well. Things had more or less smoothed out with my ex, but I still couldn't forgive my wife-in-law for taking my place. There was no logical reason for me to feel that way, but I'd been left with a shell of a life and I still held it against her. I had tried to get back at her a couple of times when I showed up at their house, once in the middle of a luncheon she was hostessing, crying hysterically and pounding on the door, demanding to see my husband.

Finally, one night, out of sheer desperation, I just got down on my knees and prayed to God for help. I confessed that I had messed up my life and stopped going to church, but that I had never really abandoned my faith. I told Him that I was lost and didn't know where to go from here.

That evening I dreamed of Job. Now I hadn't actually read the scriptures for years, but Job had everything taken away from him and endured it all with unfailing faith. In the end his life was restored and he was made whole.

Shortly thereafter I volunteered for peer counseling at a community health center and later decided to go into training to help people who are going through hard times. If I can be there for someone else, I feel like that's what I'm supposed to do on this earth. Giving to other people gives me a great deal in return. Not a day goes by that I am not thankful for some aspect of my life. Now when I do feel the occasional emptiness, I can turn to Him for comfort instead of making it my wife-in-law's burden, the way I used to.

While many women were able to pinpoint occurrences, events, or conversations that were specific turning points for them, others simply stated that time had indeed healed the wife-in-law wound. There is an old saying that time is a dressmaker specializing in alterations. A wife-in-law in one of our sessions told us that one of her many turning points had to do with a sentimental attachment to the dress she wore the day of her son's christening. For years she kept that daffodil silk shirtmaker lovingly tucked away in a Christmas box between tissue and rose sachets. Every once in a while she took it out of the box and tried it on. It remained a joyous reminder of the shared family warmth. When she was divorced, the dress became the symbol of her loss. In packing her personal belongings to leave her house for the last time, she grabbed the box and nearly tossed it in the giveaway pile. But something stopped her, and she dutifully placed it in the crate for the movers. Time passed and the memory-dress barely crossed her mind. During her last spring cleaning she came across it again, forgotten under a pile of old linens and a crocheted lap blanket. When she opened the crumpled box and looked inside, all she saw was a plain yellow dress that was a touch faded and outgrown. The time was finally right to part with it.

Every woman with whom I spoke had her own account of time and its healing effect on memories and wounds. We all have our individual ways of knowing when we have reached our milestones on the road to restored health and well-being. Emily, a first wife, experienced it this way:

> I remember reading Gail Sheehy's *Passages* after my divorce and thinking how wonderful it must be to be past this point or that but feeling that things would never get any better. But lo and behold, they did. Every year since my split-up I'm a little more hopeful. Evolution is slow and steady, and there is still a lot of residue and junk that needs to be cleaned up, but I've got the rest of my life to do it.
>
> When I reread *Passages* last year, I was delighted to realize that I had covered a lot of ground. Instead of wishing I'd get to this future point or that, I could finally say, "Thank heaven, I've passed that part!"

As time went by, other women felt less jealous of or threatened by their wives-in-law. Second-wife Norma, like Emily, was also aware of milestones. Each anniversary fortified her confidence in her marriage. At the time of our survey she had just celebrated her fourteenth wedding anniversary and was proud that she had now been married to her husband almost as long as his former wife had been. Not only did each anniversary boost her marital confidence, but her wife-in-law had finally given Norma's union her blessing. "She started to accept our marriage around year six and now I think she actually believes it is going to last!"

As time moves through the seasons of the year, nature follows a fixed law of change and transformation, but its effects endure. Personal change is similar except that we each have our own timetable, less predictable than the seasons but just as abiding. The razoring pain finally diminishes, and there is room, once again, for laughter in our lives. Kate's self-possessed outlook has reconciled the bittersweet memories of her marriage with her life as a wife-in-law.

> I will always love my first husband in a way that I think you never love again—that passionate first love. You never get over losing that, even though the man I loved so much was destroying me and my children. I knew I had to let him go, but when I left I lost a special joy that is gone forever.
>
> There are moments when I become nostalgic for all the wonderful times I left behind and brood about how my wife-in-law is enjoying them instead of me. As time goes on I know that that's simply not true. She has her marriage with all its good and bad, just as I did. At long last, I feel there is no way I'd ever really want to swap places with her.

All of these women spoke of the healing process in terms of years, not simply weeks or months. All had undergone setbacks, some more difficult than others; all had experienced fallow periods in which they felt that their lives were at a complete standstill. The encouraging fact is that women who have walked the brambled wife-in-law path swear that change for the better is possible. The pain may never be completely gone, but if we look back we can see the progress we've made despite the detours and roadblocks.

10

Don't Get Caught in the Trap!

I've always approached owner's manuals rather methodically. Before I try to put together or use a new product, I sit down and read the manual from beginning to end. With my new cellular telephone, for example, I stopped to test the various features as they were described in the manual. I've never actually used all the available features regularly enough to remember how they work, but because of my initial overview of the instructions, I know these capabilities are at my fingertips.

In much the same way, I'd like you to think of this last chapter as a "user's manual" for a more successful wife-in-law relationship. It contains eleven strategies based on the distilled wisdom of all the women who so generously participated in this research. The strategies are not listed in order of priority or effectiveness, because each is equally important and can be referred to as specific problems arise. Some strategies will be easier than others to put to use, or you may find that you're not quite ready to give up an old, familiar way of handling your wife-in-law. But each tactic has helped many women escape the traps that are so easy to fall into. So I urge you to experiment, particularly if you are eager to move on to a more comfortable relationship with the "other woman" in your life.

If you find you are already practicing most or all of them, I'd guess that you are among the lucky 40 percent who have achieved a satisfactory level of comfort in their wife-in-law relationships.

The strategies that follow represent the collective advice of both former and current wives, as well as a number of women who have found themselves in both roles. Whether we seek close, interactive relationships with our wives-in-law, or distant yet civil ones, they can guide us toward a more comfortable resolution.

Eleven Strategies for Handling the Wife-in-law Relationship
1. Allow time for healing
2. Read supportive, enlightening books
3. Find a confidant, support group, or counselor
4. Understand and accept the reality of being a wife-in-law
5. Concentrate on yourself—know yourself, take care of yourself, nurture yourself
6. Appreciate your wife-in-law's perspective
7. Keep others—especially children—out of the middle
8. Respect your wife-in-law's emotional and physical boundaries
9. Find the humor in the situation—and laugh
10. Keep the faith—and pray
11. If all else fails—fake it!

ALLOW TIME FOR HEALING:

We need only recall a physical ailment—a wound, a broken bone, the flu, major surgery—to remind ourselves that the healing process requires time. Barring terminal illness, the body moves toward health. Even in the event of permanent injury, our bodies miraculously restore themselves by strengthening unafflicted areas to compensate for weaknesses. But it all takes time. In fact, often that's all it does take.

Similarly, I believe the spirit has a natural capability to be restored, to mend, to heal—if we will just let it happen and grant it the time needed. Although the pain of wife-in-law friction can be overpowering at times, we should never allow it to become a terminal condition. If we can prevent it from taking hold of us and festering, we can ensure our recovery. But we need to respect the healing process.

We've heard from numerous women in this book about the enormous healing power of time. "Having survived the birth of my ex-husband's new son—and making it through that first year of constantly having to hear about baby Nicholas—I know I can live through anything," proclaimed one veteran wife-in-law. Others spoke of familiarity breeding more tolerance of their wife-in-law, rather than contempt. The months or years during which they adjusted to another woman's claim on their ex-husband softened the initial blow to their egos and enabled them to accept the reality of their wife-in-law predicament. These women agreed that with time comes experience and maturity, which help to ease even longstanding difficulties between wives-in-law. As we discover new ways of coping we will find that old wounds hurt less. That early pain that we feel will never go away (when we want to pull the covers over our heads and never get out of bed or cry out in the night in despair) eventually is transformed into more manageable emotions. Petty arguments and rivalries, comparisons between ourselves and the "other wife," become less important. Our emotions are less raw; life goes on in spite of everything. And we start to feel better about ourselves—often much to our own surprise.

READ SUPPORTIVE, ENLIGHTENING BOOKS:

Years ago, a librarian friend of mine taught me that the sum of library science was being able to hand the right person the right book at the right time. I've reflected fondly on her insight each time I've stumbled across a helpful article or someone has lent me the perfect book for a particularly plaguing problem.

Many of the women who contributed to this book commented with astonishment that they had happened on just the right book at the right time. Rena said that a friend's recommendation of Robin Norwood's *Women Who Love Too Much* turned out to be one of the most important turning points in her life. That book, she said, gave her the tools for living that she desperately needed and addressed her special needs at a deeply troubled time far better than the many hours she had spent in counseling.

Kate, too, talked about accidentally coming across Maxwell Maltz's *Creative Living for Today* just when she felt she was at a crossroads in her life—living in a rented house with three small children, no job, no husband. The book's ideas offered her an encouraging and more positive approach to problem solving.

When Terry's husband left to return to his former wife, she was so devastated that she literally took to her bed. One day, after she had been holed up in the house for almost a week, the doorbell rang. It was the postman with a gift from a friend, a copy of Nora Ephron's *Heartburn*—a novel about the author's discovery of her husband's infidelity. "So I crawled back into bed and read the entire book in one night. I laughed and cried so hard, and identified so strongly with the heroine, that I broke through my emotional stalemate. I finally had the strength to get out of bed—which was definitely a first step!"

Many women referred to the Bible, as well as to other inspirational works, as sources of hope and promise. Several women talked about the benefits of general reading, not only as a diversion but for personal enhancement. Edna absorbed herself in books related to her special interest in endangered rain forests and the environment, rather than dwelling on her exhausting emotional tugs-of-war with her wife-in-law. It not only took her mind off her troubles, but was enriching and rewarding in itself.

Wives-in-law found comfort, guidance, or just a good laugh in books of all categories—self-help, inspirational, humor. The

Recommended Reading section following lists some eighty-one titles specifically recommended by participants in this research as having been particularly helpful. The recommended list includes books on relationships, divorce, remarriage, marriage to divorced men, problems with parenting and stepparenting, and books addressing, more generally, larger life issues.

FIND A CONFIDANT, SUPPORT GROUP, OR COUNSELOR:

"Reach out," said Rena, "and find a friend who understands where you're coming from—someone who'll be there for you." She doesn't know what she would have done without the friends who listened to her when she needed to vent her turbulent emotions interminably. "Several of them had been there before. They really understood," she told me feelingly.

Former-wife Angela found that her friendship with Laura, whose circumstances were similar to her own, was an absolute lifesaver. She'd been divorced six years when her ex-husband remarried, and he and his new wife were expecting a baby, as was Laura's wife-in-law. Laura also has a daughter about the same age as Angela's son. The two vent their frustrations, share experiences and problems, and come up with solutions, even when none seem possible. They provide companionship for each other, and they've both learned a great deal over the years about the wife-in-law situation and its traps and pitfalls. They double their experience by swapping stories and insights.

If one friend can provide all this, networking with others who have lived through similar emotions and experiences holds boundless possibilities. Now that divorce is less a stigma and more a fact of life, joining in a support group of wives-in-law can be extremely comforting and enlightening. The women in our discussion groups often voiced their appreciation at being able to meet with others who had stumbled down the same path. They felt lucky to live in an era when problems are explored openly rather than being swept under the rug as in past generations. Most significantly, they reported that the peer group experience made plain to them that they were not alone in their struggles.

There are many ways to begin your own support group: word of mouth through friends and friends of friends; an ad in a community newspaper or magazine; posting an announcement on the bulletin board or in a newsletter of a community center, counseling center, or YWCA/YWHA. Whichever you choose, the experience is certain to be rewarding. You may find this book—as well as others listed in Recommended Reading— helpful as a starting point for your discussions. The essential purpose is to create a forum for voicing your own problems and listening to others with similar concerns.

The final component in "reaching out" is professional counseling. As I noted earlier, family counseling is particularly helpful in dealing with the issues surrounding divorce and remarriage. When other members of the family are present in therapy, the process is more immediate and direct and progress can be swifter. Instead of talking *about* your former husband or wife-in-law or teenager, you can talk *to* them in an objective, less threatening therapeutic environment. A counselor will then be able to hear from all involved parties; this overview can be enormously useful in advising or guiding each family member.

Even if other members of your family aren't willing to join you in therapy, seeing a professional counselor on your own can still be beneficial. It's extremely important for former wives to resolve their feelings toward their wives-in-law and ex-husbands, and for current wives to deal with emotional conflicts concerning stepchildren and ex-wives. Therapy can be helpful in all these instances. It can assist us in building self-esteem, so that when our wife-in-law is combative or treats us shabbily, we don't take it personally, but rather perceive her behavior as an unavoidable aspect of the wife-in-law dilemma. When we feel good about ourselves, our impulse toward retaliation gives way to a desire for compromise and resolution.

"Resolving" our feelings doesn't necessarily mean doing away with them. It means working through them to understand why we feel the way we do, how we react and relate to those who "made us" feel that way, and how we can come to terms with our own personal reality. Resolving our feelings for an ex-husband doesn't necessarily mean that we learn to stop loving—or hating and resenting—him. Resolving our feelings of jealousy toward a wife-in-law doesn't necessarily mean we stop feeling jealous or threatened.

What resolution *does* mean is that our feelings no longer control us. Kathy may still resent her ex-husband for leaving her for a younger wife, but she's no longer obsessed by her resentment. With the help of a therapist, she has worked through her anger, sadness, and disappointment and is now able to assess her life with her ex-husband more objectively. Therapy has helped her put her failed marriage and her problems with her wife-in-law in proper context. She now acknowledges that her ex-husband was a product of a dysfunctional home himself and unconsciously repeated his own father's pattern of habitual philandering and multiple marriages. She's also aware of the ways in which her expectations for a successful marriage with such a man were too naive. And, finally, she's learned that taking her disappointment and hostility out on her wife-in-law—because she's an easy target and a willing adversary—only embroils her in further stress-producing conflict. The point is, whether we do so in a therapeutic setting, in a support group, or by ourselves, resolving our feelings—acknowledging them, viewing them in perspective, understanding them, and learning over time how to deal with them—allows us to extricate ourselves from the "her versus me" trap and to move on with our lives.

Whether you communicate with a friend, a support group, or a counselor, there is help available if you need it and take advantage of it. Adjusting to a difficult wife-in-law relationship can be sheer hell, and we're entitled to all the help we can get. Holly put it this way: "I wish I understood why I needed so much personal validation, why I had to hear someone tell me I was okay, special, and not such a bad person after all. But I did have that need, and therapy helped me. Now I'm willing to reach out and help others in my wife-in-law support group."

UNDERSTAND AND ACCEPT THE REALITY OF BEING A WIFE-IN-LAW:

"Get a grip!" as one of my best friends used to counsel. Wallowing in our pain, obsessing about our wife-in-law, fixating on what really bugs us about our mutual husband, won't improve our lives. In fact, we hurt only ourselves when we concentrate on what can't be changed. We need to let go of the past and accept the present.

In our culminating sessions, we summed up with the following wise counsel: Accept the facts. Accept the end of a relationship. Accept your wife-in-law—as the new center of your ex-husband's life, as the mother of his children, as the stepmother of your kids. Accept the former family, the new family. Accept the fact that some of your old friends want to hang out with your wife-in-law instead of you. Accept the fact that you have to make new friends. Accept the imperfect money situation. Accept the reality that none of us has the best of everything. Perhaps most important, accept that hardship and pain can be instrumental to our ultimate growth. And if the impossible takes longer, and full acceptance is not achievable, try as hard as you can to accept as much as you can. None of us can do more than our best.

Tough talk from some very tough women! It's difficult enough to be a wife-in-law, much less understand your circumstances or accept your pain, but the advice from the experts—those who have walked in the very same shoes that are killing you right now—is that unless we do precisely that, continued misery is guaranteed.

From an ex-wife: "The day we learn to let go and accept the end of a marital relationship that went bad is probably the day we will begin to be better parents to our children."

And from a current wife: "There needs to be a voice of reason. You need to understand that you're not marrying just one person, but two or three or four. Stop and think whether this is a situation you really want to live with. Understand that you'll have to deal with this for the rest of your life."

In other words, we can't fight reality. We must begin to make changes in our life based on the existent situation. Your wife-in-law is not going to go away. Your ex-husband *is* gone. He is not going to suddenly return; he is not going to become a model father if he never was one before. Your stepchildren aren't going to love and trust you from Day One. And no one is going to come and miraculously "save" any of us from the obstacles we face. But when we do our best to be objective and honest about our lives, and try to understand what has happened to us and why, we begin to be able to take control of our own lives.

CONCENTRATE ON YOURSELF—KNOW YOURSELF, TAKE CARE OF YOURSELF, NURTURE YOURSELF:

Understanding and accepting our circumstances allows us to begin to take care of ourselves. It's difficult to get into this mind-set, since most of us, even in this "Me First" decade, have been brought up to be care givers, to look after others first and ourselves last. But the warning from the wives-in-law with whom I communicated was that if we don't want to self-destruct, we're going to have to put more emphasis on ourselves.

According to the women in this research, looking after ourselves begins with forgiveness—first forgiving ourselves for failures or faults, and then forgiving others who may have hurt us. When we learn to forgive, we can finally let go of the emotions which disable us.

Once we overcome the often obsessive need to blame others (sometimes justified, sometimes not), when we stop reliving old scenarios and blaming ourselves, we can finally move forward and discover and nurture our special attributes and potentials. This is an essential step in the never-ending process of personal growth.

Another crucial aspect of learning to take care of ourselves is financial self-sufficiency, however long the process takes. For a minority of women—those who are beyond middle age and have never worked outside the home—this may be difficult, if not impossible. But without financial independence, I don't believe we can reach our fullest potential as women or, indeed, as human beings. Unless we're able to support ourselves, we will always somehow "belong" to someone else. Yet, ironically, knowing that we don't *need* a mate for financial reasons frees us to develop a sounder, more meaningful intimate relationship. Even for that minority of wives-in-law who have never worked outside the home, there's still the possibility of developing a part-time independent income, however small. In fact, "homemaker" skills can often be transformed into money-making ventures. An earned income—whether it comes from a part-time job as a reader at the children's library or selling homemade muffins to the local gourmet café—goes a long way toward building self-esteem.

Part of nurturing ourselves is developing our special interests and curiosities about the world. There's nothing like swimming with sea lions, or helping out on a peace initiative, or taking that course in the Middle Ages to give us a whole new perspective on ourselves. As we become more interested in life and the world around us and in other people's problems, we become more interesting to others, and more important, to ourselves. We feel ourselves stretching. We like ourselves better. We enjoy our own company. We take pride in our new knowledge and achievements. And we gradually discover that we are less concerned about the things that used to drive us wild with jealousy and bitterness. We learn to rise above the pettiness of wife-in-law squabbles, if for no other reason than we've found better, more important things to do.

APPRECIATE YOUR WIFE-IN-LAW'S PERSPECTIVE:

It wasn't until I formed a close relationship with a professional colleague who is a second wife and heard her talk about her frustrations with her wife-in-law, her responsibilities as a stepmother, and her concerns for her own child born into the second marriage, that I truly appreciated the complexities of being a second wife. I had focused until then solely on the unhappy state of the ex-wife—my own condition. Until my friendship with her, I assumed second wives more or less had it made—they had "custody" of the mutual husband, their futures were secure, and they'd live happily ever after. I had dwelt on my own problems so intensely that I had never really given much thought to the "other wife's" concerns.

It was in comparing my own perspective with my friend's current-wife situation that I realized all wives-in-law have emotional and practical issues with which they must wrestle. And it was that realization that inspired me to write this book.

I hope the stories in this book have given you a much deeper understanding and empathy for the separate yet equally difficult roles of both current and former wives. Your ability to extend that understanding to your own wife-in-law is, of course, a greater challenge. Many of the wives-in-law in our study shared my experience; they spoke of having finally grasped the "opposing" wife-in-law perspective only when they had a friend or relative in that role.

When we can envision someone we care about in the role inhabited by our "adversary"—our own wife-in-law—we begin to feel less adversarial. That's not to say the issues or the rivalries fade away, but it does mean that compromise becomes possible. The greater our understanding of the wife-in-law relationship, the more we learn to see our own wife-in-law as a real person and treat her accordingly. As corny as it may sound, many wives-in-law told me their basic strategy for dealing with the "other wife" is the Golden Rule: "I try to treat her as I want to be treated."

Another piece of advice from the women in this study is to remember that your wife-in-law is a person *separate from* your mutual husband. Both current and former wives admitted blaming their wives-in-law for his shortcomings and ill treatment. Former wives blame current ones when mutual husbands are late with child support checks, when children are ignored during weekend visits, and in numerous other circumstances which we've explored in the course of this book. Curent wives blame former ones when mutual husbands accuse them of having all the former wife's flaws. Not only is this unfair to the wife-in-law, it lets the man off the hook and leaves any thorny issues unresolved. Similarly, when we vent certain feelings on our wife-in-law that are really meant for our mutual husband, we're communicating with the wrong person and often failing to face important emotional issues. Appreciating your wife-in-law's perspective includes letting *her* off the hook when it comes to problems that aren't her fault or of her making.

KEEP OTHERS—ESPECIALLY CHILDREN—OUT OF THE MIDDLE:

Try as we may, no matter how we handle things, others—especially children—always seem to be caught in the middle. Friends and family members have options for greater or lesser involvement in the wife-in-law conflict; they can become scarce, withdraw, choose sides, or flee altogether. Children, particularly young children, cannot. They are wedged between the two families.

As we learned in Chapter 4, children are used as messengers, mediators, and emotional hostages and, like all innocent bystanders, can suffer the consequences of existing hostilities. If I had to choose one message to communicate to every wife-in-law reading this book, it would be to do everything in your power to keep the children out of the middle. However hurt or angry or resentful we feel, our children are not responsible. Forcing them to carry negative messages back and forth is very harmful to them.

You don't have to be fond of—or even like—your wife-in-law, but it's important to remember that she's still your children's stepmother or your stepchild's mother, and every child deserves to have happy, healthy home relationships. Children and stepchildren are entitled to their own feelings and judgments. If you don't give them the necessary space, they may suffer grievously for it. If you do, they are likely to develop self-esteem and the ability to trust themselves, qualities which will be invaluable throughout their lives.

Another reason for keeping children out of the middle is to let yourself confront your own conflicts and emotions. If you use your kids to run interference between you and your wife-in-law or your mutual husband, you are shielding yourself from your own feelings. The emotions you suppress, the "secrets" you keep from yourself and others, can be paralyzing; they can prevent you from moving on with your life.

RESPECT YOUR WIFE-IN-LAW'S EMOTIONAL AND PHYSICAL BOUNDARIES:

Inherent in the wife-in-law relationship are very real implicit and explicit boundaries, both physical and emotional. Closely related to appreciating your wife-in-law's perspective, respecting her boundaries can make or break a workable relationship.

Often a boundary can be as simple as not calling your wife-in-law's house after 10:00 P.M.—or as specific as knowing "your place" in the receiving line at your stepdaughter's wedding. The question of boundaries frequently comes up around special family events, as we've learned throughout the course of this book—a stepmother is told, explicitly or indirectly, that she's not welcome at a stepson's birthday party given by his maternal grandmother; or an ex-wife is barred from attending her ex-mother-in-law's funeral. Our feelings may be wounded by such territorial proscriptions, but we need to remember that we each have our own set of "limits" as well as the right to expect our wife-in-law to respect them.

We all need to feel that we have some control over our own lives, some power to determine how we want to interact with others. Allowing your wife-in-law to set limits on her relationship with you—and informing her of yours—will be beneficial to both of you.

We've heard from wives-in-law who were great pals yet drew

the line when it came to talking about their mutual husband—especially about intimate information. Wives-in-law who didn't enjoy such closeness set the boundaries at their front doorstep—neither ever venturing into the other's home. Women with children seemed extremely concerned about time boundaries—keeping time-clock tabs on visitation schedules so that the allotted time with their children or stepchildren wasn't infringed upon. They cherished their time with their kids and made it clear to their wives-in-law that it was not to be cut into except in emergencies.

Certain parenting issues also involve setting and respecting limits. Several former wives said they didn't want their wives-in-law to discuss sexuality with their kids. Some drew the line when it came to advising their older kids about college or careers. Then there were stepmothers who refused to take on the burden of talking to stepchildren about basic discipline, demanding that their wives-in-law clue their children in before they spent time in the "second" home.

When it comes to drawing boundaries, there are no universal standards to apply; the rules differ from one situation to another. The important thing is to acknowledge and respect your wife-in-law's lines of demarcation. The difficulty lies in the fact that we rarely discuss our preferred limits until after infringements have been committed.

FIND THE HUMOR IN THE SITUATION—AND LAUGH:

Mark Twain may have had wives-in-law in mind when he observed, "The secret source of humor itself is not joy, but sorrow." Actually, it is a joy when we find humor in our personal sorrow and are able to laugh—sometimes cynically, sometimes halfheartedly, sometimes uproariously. In fact, the sources of our conflict and pain are identical to the sources of our humor and laughter: our children, our finances, our mutual spouse, our shared in-laws and friends, our property, and even ourselves. As Kate pointed out, "We know we're making progress when we can laugh at those very things that used to make us cry."

Almost half the women in this study said that their wives-in-law had become a source of laughter. Some described this laughter as genuine and friendly, an expression of mutual sympathy for shared situations or problems. Others spoke of the laughter as being a cynical response to "cruel and unusual wife-in-law punishment." Many used laughter as a weapon to retaliate: "I sure have lots of laughs at her expense," said Wilma.

Sometimes we laugh because there's simply no other appropriate response—as when Beth's wife-in-law asked to borrow the money Beth and her husband had received as an anniversary gift from her parents!

The physical and emotional benefits of laughter have been well documented and are credited for accelerating recovery from illness and extending our days on the planet. Wives-in-law must learn when to take a situation seriously and when to laugh it off. The ticket is to learn to relax, shrug off petty matters, find humor wherever we can—and laugh!

KEEP THE FAITH—AND PRAY:

Just as it was impossible to talk about handling the wife-in-law relationship and other divorce fallout without talking about professional help, it became impossible to talk about the resolution of these issues without talking about the search for inner resources, spirituality, and an active, living faith.

Personally, I've faced many days when I wasn't sure how I could possibly make it through until bedtime; days when I was totally consumed by deep sadness and grief; days when the responsibilities of my life were completely overwhelming.

Yet somehow or other I always got through; and I eventually recognized that I hadn't been going it alone. I had reached deep into my past, to the lessons of my childhood, and found a special comfort, a special knowledge, a special trust. What I had discovered—or rediscovered—was a very special personal faith in God and His purposes. That faith became a reservoir of strength for me.

I sometimes remark in jest that my knees have become

calloused over the past ten years from the hours spent in prayer. Actually, the only reason they're not is because most of my prayers have been muttered on the run—standing in a grocery line, sitting in the doctor's office, walking the dog, swimming, driving my son to school. But God has not let me down. He has been there for me and has answered my simple, urgent prayers for strength, guidance, and direction, and for forgiveness.

And so I join the many other women who have shared their stories here in urging others to do whatever is needed to stay in touch with or rediscover their own source of inner strength. However we define it, that "peace that passes understanding" is an invaluable resource.

IF ALL ELSE FAILS—FAKE IT!

On a recent vacation trip to South America, I spent some dozen or so very frustrating hours in the Miami airport attempting to locate my luggage, which had somehow become lost between Knoxville, Atlanta, and Miami. Locating it was particularly important to me on that trip, for I would be arriving in the Ecuadorean capital city of Quito late one evening and proceeding early the following morning for a week's journey on the Amazon River. My traveling suit and white high heels truly wouldn't cut it—and there would be no shopping time in Quito to replace my "jungle" wardrobe before boarding the flight for the interior. I simply had to find my luggage!

As one negative report followed another, I began to lose heart and laid a contingency plan: an early Sunday morning shopping spree at the nearest Miami discount store for some basic clothes to get me through a week on the Amazon.

Upon checking in for the flight to Quito the next morning, with my quickly assembled new wardrobe in hand, I learned, yet again, that there was no sign of my luggage. "When you arrive in Quito," the airline representative said to me, "pass through immigration and then just proceed with the other passengers to the baggage area and *pretend* your luggage is there."

Pretend my luggage would be in the baggage area in Quito,

when, according to all reports, it had vanished from the face of the earth? Was this woman losing her mind? As we approached the gate in the final boarding minutes, the airline agent hailed us down to say that—*voilà!*—my luggage had been found, was on board the plane, and would indeed be in the baggage area in Quito. And it was.

I often reflect on the wizardry of that flight representative who advised me so seriously to proceed to the baggage area and *pretend* my luggage would be there. And after all the anxiety, confusion, and frenzied shopping, there it was. And I have to admit that I've adopted this South American pretend-your-luggage-will-be-there philosophy. And, by golly, as often as not, it works. I now say wholeheartedly, when all else fails—or when it's only partially working—fake it! Just pretend your luggage will be there, and maybe it will. Pretend your wife-in-law isn't driving you up the wall with her demands or her insensitivity, and maybe she won't.

After all, this is the basis of a good many "positive thinking" philosophies. When you treat your "enemy" with courtesy and respect, her behavior may begin to mirror yours, and soon your grudges become a little less hardened. And so do theirs . . .

I maintain a strong belief in the power of self-fulfilling prophecies. Visualize things happening in a certain way, and there's a good chance they will. You say you can't get rid of those emotions which are consuming you? Fake it. Pretend they're not consuming you. You say you can't find forgiveness in your heart for yourself or your wife-in-law or your mutual husband? Fake it. Pretend you forgive them. Then, in six or twelve months, pause and take a look back and see how far you've come; I bet you'll be pleasantly surprised.

Change doesn't happen overnight—or even after one or two pleasant chats with your wife-in-law. Even if we were able to implement all eleven strategies overnight, our wives-in-law would still get on our nerves on occasion, we'd still get the blues once in a while, and we'd still lie awake nights wondering how to juggle two divided yet connected households. The women in this research have taught me to take strength in knowing others have been there. They struggle with less-than-perfect lives, but as time goes on, the struggle eases. By learning to communicate, by gaining an overall perspective, by valuing themselves, they become adept at avoiding the "adversary trap"—they no longer need to make their wife-in-law the bad guy in order to feel in control of their own lives.

Eventually, most of us find that the "other wife" who used to be the focus of emotions ranging from irritation to agony isn't as threatening as she once was. She may not be our best friend or our confidant or our bosom buddy, but she's not necessarily our adversary either. She is just—our wife-in-law!

✻ NOTES ✻

CHAPTER ONE:
1. U.S. Department of Commerce. *Statistical Abstract of the United States.* Bureau of the Census. Washington, D.C., 1989.
2. Larry Bumpass. *Changing Family Patterns in the United States.* Paper presented at the Census Analysis Workshop: Families and Households, Data and Trends. October 1–2, 1987. Madison, Wisconsin.
3. National Center for Health Statistics. *Monthly Vital Statistics Report,* "Advance Report of Final Marriage Statistics, 1986." Vol. 38, No. 3. Supplement 2, July 13, 1989, p. 13.

CHAPTER TWO:
1. J. A. Sweet and Larry Bumpass. *American Families and Households.* New York: Russell Sage Foundation, 1987.

CHAPTER NINE:
1. A. J. Norton and J. E. Moorman. *Current Media Issues in Marriage and Divorce.* Paper presented at the Census Analysis Workshop: Families and Households, Data and Trends. October 1–2, 1987. Madison, Wisconsin.

✳ RECOMMENDED READING ✳

The books listed below are those specifically recommended by the women we interviewed. All of the books here were noted for being particularly helpful to the personal decisions and growth processes surrounding divorce, remarriage, and marriage to a divorced man. (Titles are listed alphabetically.)

Melody Beattie. *Beyond Codependency.* Harper & Row.
Bible, The, various translations, various publishers.
Ralph F. Ranier. *Blended Families: A Guide for Stepparents.* Liguori Publications.
Richard Bach. *Bridge Across Forever.* Dell/Morrow.
Jay E. Adams. *Christian Living in the Home.* Baker Books.
Colette Dowling. *Cinderella Complex: Women's Hidden Fear of Independence.* Pocket Books.
Melody Beattie. *Codependent No More.* Harper & Row.
Foundation for Inner Peace. *Course in Miracles.*
Abigail Trafford. *Crazy Time: Surviving Divorce.* Bantam.
Mel Krantzler. *Creative Divorce.* M. Evans, Lippincott.
Maxwell Maltz. *Creative Living for Today.* Pocket Books.
Shakti Gawain. *Creative Visualization.* Bantam.
Harriet G. Lerner. *Dance of Anger: A Woman's Guide to Changing the Patterns of Intimate Relationships.* Harper & Row.
Harriet G. Lerner. *Dance of Intimacy: A Woman's Guide to Courageous Acts of Change in Key Relationships.* Harper & Row.
Constance R. Ahrons. *Divorced Families.* W. W. Norton.
Paul Bilheimer. *Don't Waste Your Sorrows.* Bethany House.
Norman Vincent Peale. *Dynamic Imaging.* Revell.
Rodegast, Pat, and Judith Stanton. *Emmanuel's Book: A Manual for Living Comfortably in the Cosmos.* Bantam.
David Augsburger. *Freedom of Forgiveness, The.* Moody.
Anne Morrow Lindbergh. *Gift from the Sea.* Walker & Co.
Stephen Levine. *Gradual Awakening, A.* Doubleday.

Helen G. Brown. *Having It All.* Pocket Books.
Nora Ephron. *Heartburn.* Pocket Books.
Merle Shain. *Hearts That We Broke Long Ago.* Bantam.
John Powell. *He Touched Me: My Pilgrimage of Prayer.* Tabor Publications.
Mildred Newman, and Bernard Berkowitz. *How to Be Your Own Best Friend.* Ballantine.
Marcia Hootman, and Pat Perkins. *How to Forgive Your Ex-husband.* Warner Books.
Eugene Walder. *How to Get Out of an Unhappy Marriage or an Unhappy Relationship.* Putnam.
Melba Colgrove. *How to Survive the Loss of a Love.* Bantam.
Jess Lair. *I Ain't Much, Baby, But I'm All I've Got.* Fawcett.
Jess Lair. *I Ain't Well—But I Sure Am Better: Mutual Need.* Fawcett.
David P. Campbell. *If You Don't Know Where You're Going—You'll Probably End Up Somewhere Else.* Tabor Publications.
Richard Bach. *Illusions: The Adventures of a Reluctant Messiah.* Dell.
Thomas A. Harris. *I'm O.K., You're O.K.* Avon.
Alan Paton. *Instrument of Thy Peace.* Walker & Co.
Lillian B. Rubin. *Intimate Strangers.* Harper & Row.
Richard Bach. *Jonathan Livingston Seagull.* Walker & Co.
Robert Skutch. *Journey Without Distance.* Celestial Arts.
Ruth Roosevelt. *Living in Step.* McGraw-Hill.
Leo F. Buscaglia. *Living, Loving, and Learning.* Fawcett.
Ann Kaiser Stearns. *Living Through Personal Crisis.* Ballantine.
Leo F. Buscaglia. *Love.* Fawcett.
Gerald Jampolsky. *Love Is Letting Go of Fear.* Bantam.
Leo F. Buscaglia. *Loving Each Other.* Fawcett.
Sonya Friedman. *Men Are Just Desserts.* Warner Books.
Forward, Susan, and Joan Torres. *Men Who Hate Women and the Women Who Love Them.* Bantam.
Judith Viorst. *Necessary Losses.* Fawcett.
Penny Penderson. *On My Way to Love.* Hallmark.
Stewart Emery. *Owners Manual for Your Life, The.* Pocket Books.
Gail Sheehy. *Passages.* Bantam.
M. Scott Peck. *People of the Lie: The Hope for Healing Human Evil.* Simon and Schuster.
Frank Main. *Perfect Parenting and Other Myths: New Ways to Encourage Responsible, Cooperative & Happy Children.* CompCare Publications.
Norman V. Peale. *Power of Positive Thinking.* Prentice Hall.

Helen H. Perlman. *Relationship: The Heart of Helping People.* University of Chicago Press.

M. Scott Peck. *Road Less Traveled, The.* (Touchstone Books) Simon & Schuster.

John Powell. *Secret of Staying in Love, The.* Tabor Publications.

Hermann Hesse. *Siddhartha.* Buccaneer Books.

Keith and Andrea Wells Miller. *Single Experience, The.* Word Books.

Cowan, Connell, and Melvyn Kinder. *Smart Women, Foolish Choices: Finding the Right Men & Avoiding the Wrong Ones.* Crown.

Merle Shain. *Some Men Are More Perfect Than Others.* Bantam.

Amy B. and Thomas A. Harris. *Staying Okay.* Avon.

Elizabeth Einstein. *Stepfamily: Living, Loving & Learning, The.* Macmillan.

Nancy Thayer. *Stepping.* Doubleday.

Charles R. Swindoll. *Strike the Original Match.* Multnomah.

John R. Price. *Superbeings, The.* Quartus Books.

Gerald G. Jampolsky. *Teach Only Love: The Seven Principles of Attitudinal Healing.* Bantam.

Charles R. Swindoll. *Three Steps Forward—Two Steps Back.* Bantam.

William Bridges. *Transitions: Making Sense of Life's Changes.* Addison-Wesley.

Gerald and Myrna Silver. *Weekend Fathers.* Berkley Publications.

Dr. Joyce Brothers. *What Every Woman Should Know About Men.* Ballantine.

Merle Shain. *When Lovers Are Friends.* Bantam.

John Powell. *Why Am I Afraid to Love?* Tabor Publications.

John Powell. *Why Am I Afraid to Tell You Who I Am?* Tabor Publications.

Penelope Russianoff. *Why Do I Think I'm Nothing Without a Man?* Bantam.

Melia, Jinx, and Pauline Lyttle. *Why Jenny Can't Lead: Understanding the Male Dominant System.* Op. Politics.

Frederick Buechner. *Wishful Thinking: A Theological ABC.* Harper & Row.

Marilyn French. *Women's Room, The.* Jove Publications.

Kevin Leman. *Women Who Can't Say No & the Men Who Control Them.* Dell.

Robin Norwood. *Women Who Love Too Much.* Pocket Books.

Darian B. Cooper. *You Can Be the Wife of a Happy Husband.* Victor Books.

Herb Cohen. *You Can Negotiate Anything.* Lyle Stuart.

* BIBLIOGRAPHY *

Bumpass, Larry. *Changing Family Patterns in the United States.* Paper presented at the Census Analysis Workshop: Families and Households, Data and Trends. October 1–2, 1987. Madison, Wisconsin.

Cherlin, Andrew J. *Marriage, Divorce, Remarriage.* Cambridge, MA: Harvard University Press, 1981.

Fisher, Roger and Scott Brown. *Getting Together: Building a Relationship That Gets to Yes.* Boston: Houghton Mifflin Co., 1988.

Goldscheider, F. K. *Consequences of Changes in Household and Family Structure.* Paper presented at the Census Analysis Workshop: Families and Households, Data and Trends. October 1–2, 1987. Madison, Wisconsin.

Moorman, J. E. *Current Media Issues in Marriage and Divorce.* Paper presented at the Census Analysis Workshop: Families and Households, Data and Trends. October 1–2, 1987. Madison, Wisconsin.

National Center for Health Statistics. "Advance Report of Final Divorce Statistics, 1985." *Monthly Vital Statistics Report,* Vol. 36, No. 8. Supp. DHHS Pub. No. (PHS) 88-1120. Public Health Service. Hyattsville, MD. December 7, 1987.

National Center for Health Statistics. "Advance Report of Final Marriage Statistics, 1985." *Monthly Vital Statistics Report,* DHHS, Vol. 37, No. 1, Supplement, April 29, 1988.

National Center for Health Statistics. "Advance Report of Final Marriage Statistics, 1986." *Monthly Vital Statistics Report,* Vol. 38, No. 3. Supplement, July 13, 1989.

National Center for Health Statistics. "Annual Summary of Births, Marriages, Divorces, and Deaths. United States, 1987." *Monthly Vital Statistics Report,* Vol. 36, No. 13. DHHS Pub. No. (PHS) 88-1120. Public Health Service, Hyattsville, MD. July 29, 1988.

National Center for Health Statistics. "First Marriages, United States, 1968–1976," *Vital and Health Statistics,* DHEW, Series 21, No. 35, September 1979.

Norton, A. J. and Moorman, J. E. "Current Trends in Marriage and Divorce Among American Women." *Journal of Marriage and the Family,* Vol. 49 (February 1987), pp. 3–14.

Pettit, E. J. and Bloom, B. L. "Whose Decision Was It? The Effects of

Initiator Status on Adjustment to Marital Disruption." *Journal of Marriage and the Family*, Vol. 46 (August 1984), pp. 587–595.

Sweet, J. A. and Bumpass, L. L. *American Families and Households.* New York: Russell Sage Foundation, 1987.

U.S. Bureau of the Census, Current Population Reports, Series P-20, No. 423. *Marital Status and Living Arrangements: March 1987.* U.S. Government Printing Office, Washington, D.C., 1988.

U.S. Bureau of the Census, Current Population Reports, Series P-25, No. 1017. *Projections of the Population of States by Age, Sex, and Race: 1988 to 2010.* U.S. Government Printing Office, Washington, D.C., October 1988, Table 5.

U.S. Bureau of the Census, Current Population Reports, Series P-25, No. 1022. *U.S. Population Estimates by Age, Sex, and Race 1980 to 1987.* U.S. Government Printing Office, Washington, D.C., March 1988, Table 2.

U.S. Department of Commerce. Bureau of the Census. *Statistical Abstract of the United States.* Washington, D.C., 1989.

Wallerstein, Judith S. and Sandra Blakeslee. *Second Chances: Men, Women & Children a Decade After Divorce.* New York: Ticknor & Fields, 1989.

Weitzman, L. J. *The Divorce Revolution.* New York: Free Press, 1985.

* APPENDIX *

Wife-in-Law Trap Survey Questionnaire

Following is the survey questionnaire that formed the basis for this book. If you share a wife-in-law relationship, you may be interested in completing the questionnaire and comparing your responses to those discussed in the book.

I. BACKGROUND INFORMATION

1. Number of years your mutual husband was/has been married to you:
   ____ Years ____ Months
2. Number of years your mutual husband was/has been in his former/current marriage: ____ Years ____ Months
3. In the former marriage, the marriage between you and your mutual husband, who asked for the divorce? ____ Why? _____
4. How long ago was the divorce? ____ Years ____ Months
5. How long was your mutual husband single before his remarriage?
   ____ Years ____ Months
6. Was his current wife/were you a factor in the breakup of your marriage?
   ____ No ____ Yes
7. a. Where do you live? (City/State) _____
   b. Where does your wife-in-law live? (City/State) _____
   c. How many miles apart do you estimate these cities are? _____
   d. If you live in a different city from your wife-in-law, who moved from the location of the first marriage and why (e.g., after the divorce, did you move away for career reasons, or to be closer to your family)? _____
8. Is the former wife/are you remarried? ____ No ____ Yes

9. Whose last name do you/does the former wife use?
___ Your mutual husband's name
___ Your/Her maiden name
___ The name of a subsequent/current spouse
___ Other (Specify:) _____

10. Number of children involved:
(a) Ages of children you had with mutual husband _____
(b) Ages of children current/former wife had with mutual husband
_____
(c) Other involved children and their relationship _____

11. Ages: Yours ___ , Your mutual husband's ___ , Your wife-in-law's ___

12. Occupations: Yours _____ Your mutual husband's _____
Your wife-in-law's _____

13. Have you met your wife-in-law? ___ No ___ Yes. If yes, were you acquainted with her while she was married to/before she became involved with your mutual husband? _____

14. Describe your first meeting or conversation with your wife-in-law.
_____

15. Describe the circumstances under which you learned that your former husband intended to remarry or had remarried (for former wives only).
_____

16. Was there a particular event or occasion during which you realized that having a wife-in-law would have a significant impact on your life? Explain. _____

17. What background do you feel is pertinent to understanding the particular relationship you have with your wife-in-law?
_____

18. Please explain any unique circumstances of your wife-in-law situation. For example, are you and your wife-in-law former or current friends or do you belong to the same organizations?
_____

II. COMMUNICATIONS WITH WIFE-IN-LAW

1. How often do you communicate with your wife-in-law?
   (a) Frequently   ____ times per week
   (b) Fairly frequently   ____ times per month
   (c) Infrequently   ____ times per year
   Other (Specify:) _____

2. What are the primary issues that require you to communicate with your wife-in-law?
   ____ Finances   ____ Children
   ____ Mutual husband   ____ Other (Specify:) _____

3. What are the primary areas of conflict with your wife-in-law?
   ____ Finances   ____ Children
   ____ Mutual husband   ____ No real conflicts
   ____ Other (Specify:) _____

4. How often do you try to see things from your wife-in-law's perspective?
   ____ Practically never   ____ Rarely   ____ Sometimes
   ____ Usually   ____ Practically always
   Comments: _____

5. How often does she try to see things from your perspective?
   ____ Practically never   ____ Rarely   ____ Sometimes
   ____ Usually   ____ Practically always
   Comments: _____

6. What are the primary means of communicating with your wife-in-law?
   ____ By telephone   ____ By written correspondence
   ____ In person, one on one (privately)
   ____ In the presence of significant others (for example, at gatherings of family and friends)
   ____ In public places like restaurants or the supermarket (e.g., when you "run into each other")
   ____ Through family members (husband, children, etc.)
   ____ Other (Specify:) _____ Comments: _____

7. In general, how would you describe your communications with your wife-in-law?

____ Cordial   ____ Forced

____ Comfortable   ____ Uncomfortable

____ Other (Specify:) _____ Comments: _____

8. On which of the following "public" occasions have you interacted with—or do you anticipate interacting with—your wife-in-law?

Have   Anticipate

Interacted   Interacting

_____   _____ Adult social events (Country club, restaurants, ballet, etc.)

_____   _____ School activities and events (PTA committees, open houses, graduation exercises, etc.)

_____   _____ Special family events (Weddings, christenings, funerals, etc.)

_____   _____ Holidays and birthdays

_____   _____ Other (Specify:) _____

III. FEELINGS

1. How do you feel (or do you anticipate feeling) about "public appearances" with your wife-in-law?

____ Extremely uncomfortable   ____ Slightly uncomfortable

____ Moderately comfortable   ____ Completely comfortable

Comments: _____

2. In general, how do you feel about your wife-in-law?

____ Jealous   ____ Resentful ____ Bitter   ____ Sympathetic

____ Competitive ____ Fond   ____ Curious

____ Other (Specify:) _____ Comments: _____

3. How do you think your wife-in-law feels about you?

___ Jealous ___ Resentful ___ Bitter ___ Sympathetic

___ Competitive ___ Fond ___ Curious

___ Other (Specify:) _____

Comments: _____

4. How would you best describe the intensity of your feelings about your wife-in-law?

___ Lukewarm ___ Intense ___ Obsessed ___ Insignificant

___ Warm ___ Other (Specify:) _____

Comments: _____

5. What is your greatest frustration in dealing with your wife-in-law? Why?

_____

6. What is the most pleasant aspect in dealing with your wife-in-law? Why?

_____

7. To what degree do you feel bonded to your wife-in-law?

___ Not at all ___ Somewhat ___ Greatly

Comments: _____

8. Do you ever wonder what kind of relationship your mutual husband has/had with your wife-in-law? (For example, how they deal/dealt with their children, what they do/did for recreation, their sexual activities, etc.?) If so, what kinds of things cross your mind?

_____

9. How often do you think about your wife-in-law?

___ Almost never ___ Only when necessary to interact

___ Weekly ___ Daily ___ Many times a day

Comments: _____

10. Has your wife-in-law ever made you cry? ___ Yes ___ No

Explain: _____

11. Has your wife-in-law ever made you laugh? ___ Yes ___ No

Explain: _____

IV. ASSESSMENT OF SELF AND WIFE-IN-LAW

1. To what extent, and in what ways, are you and your wife-in-law alike?

   ____ Very much alike   ____ Somewhat alike

   ____ Basically different   ____ Complete opposites

        Comments: _____

2. What qualities do you think attracted your mutual husband to you?

   _____

3. What qualities do you think attracted your mutual husband to your wife-in-law?

   _____

4. What qualities in your mutual husband attracted you to him?

   _____

5. What qualities in your mutual husband attracted your wife-in-law to him?

   _____

6. In general, how do you compare with your wife-in-law in the following areas?

I'm Better	I'm Worse	We're About the Same	Don't Know	
____	____	____	____	Personal happiness
____	____	____	____	Professional success
____	____	____	____	Intelligence
____	____	____	____	Educational background
____	____	____	____	Talent
____	____	____	____	Social & economic background
____	____	____	____	Personality
____	____	____	____	Sexuality
____	____	____	____	Range of interests

_____ _____ _____ _____ Physical appearance
_____ _____ _____ _____ Ability to parent
_____ _____ _____ _____ Determination
_____ _____ _____ _____ Sense of humor
_____ _____ _____ _____ Openness/honesty
_____ _____ _____ _____ Ability to meet needs of hus-
band
_____ _____ _____ _____ Other (Specify:) _____

7. Do you think your mutual husband's friends and family feel closer to you or to your wife-in-law?
   (a) Friends: ____ closer to me ____ closer to wife-in-law
   (b) Family: ____ closer to me ____ closer to wife-in-law

8. Do you have any nicknames for your wife-in-law that you use to refer to her when she's not around?
   ____ Yes ____ No Specify: _____

9. Are you aware of any nicknames your wife-in-law uses to refer to you?
   ____ Yes ____ No Specify: _____

V. RELATIONSHIP QUESTIONS

1. In general, how would you say you handle your relationship with your wife-in-law, all things considered?
   ____ Very capably ____ About as well as can be expected
   ____ Very poorly
   Comments: _____

2. In general, how would you describe the overall nature of your relationship with your wife-in-law?
   ____ Comfortable ____ Uncomfortable ____ Friendly
   ____ Belligerent ____ Cordial ____ Awkward
   ____ Tense ____ Confrontational ____ Other (Specify:)
   Comments: _____

VI. RELATIONSHIP OF OTHERS TO WIFE-IN-LAW

1. What are your primary sources of information about your wife-in-law:
    ___ Firsthand knowledge/experience ___ From mutual husband
    ___ From the children ___ From mutual friends
    ___ Total strangers/acquaintances/business associates
    ___ Other (Specify:) _____
2. Do you share mutual friends with your wife-in-law (active friendships)?
    ___ Yes ___ No Comments: _____
3. What is your mutual husband's role in your relationship with your wife-in-law?
    ___ Mediator ___ Instigator of conflict ___ Noninvolvement
    ___ Other (Specify:) _____
4. How do you think your mutual husband feels about the relationship between you and your wife-in-law?
    ___ Uninvolved ___ Not at all comfortable
    ___ Somewhat comfortable ___ Very comfortable
    Comments: _____
5. In general, how do you speak of your wife-in-law to:
    (a) your children?
    ___ Favorably ___ Unfavorably ___ I don't mention her
    ___ Other (Specify:) _____
    (b) your friends?
    ___ Favorably ___ Unfavorably ___ I don't mention her
    ___ Other (Specify:) _____
    (c) her children?
    ___ Favorably ___ Unfavorably ___ I don't mention her
    ___ Other (Specify:) _____
    (d) your mutual husband?
    ___ Favorably ___ Unfavorably ___ I don't mention her
    ___ Other (Specify:) _____

(e) other members of your mutual husband's family? (e.g., parents, grandparents, etc.)

_____ Favorably   _____ Unfavorably   _____ I don't mention her

_____ Other (Specify:) _____

VII. IMPACT ON LIFESTYLE

1. In what ways has your lifestyle changed since your divorce from/ marriage to your mutual husband?

	Better	Worse	Same
a) Financially			
b) Amount of leisure time			
c) Social position			
d) Sex life			
e) General well-being			

Comments: _____

2. How has your wife-in-law's lifestyle changed since her divorce from/marriage to your mutual husband?

	Better	Worse	Same	Don't Know
a) Financially				
b) Amount of leisure time				
c) Social position				
d) Sex life				
e) General well-being				

Comments: _____

3. How do you feel about your attitude toward your current situation (legal, social, financial, etc.)?

_____ Accepting _____ Refuse to accept _____ Determined to change

Comments: _____.

VIII. DIRECTION OF WIFE-IN-LAW RELATIONSHIP

1. How important is it to you to try to have a good relationship with your wife-in-law?

Very   Not
Important   Important
   10   9   8   7   6   5   4   3   2   1

2. How important do you think it is to your wife-in-law that the two of you have a good relationship?

Very   Not
Important   Important
   10   9   8   7   6   5   4   3   2   1

3. How important is it to your mutual husband that you and your wife-in-law have a good relationship?

Very   Not
Important   Important
   10   9   8   7   6   5   4   3   2   1

4. Looking back, would you do things differently in your relationship with your wife-in-law?

____ No   ____ Yes   Comments: _____

5. How has your relationship with your wife-in-law changed over the years?

6. Are there any particular events which were turning points in the relationship?

7. How would you change your relationship if you could?

8. What advice would you give others who share a wife-in-law relationship?

9. Are there any other comments you would care to add?